NATURAL WONDERS OF GEORGIA

NATURAL WONDERS OF GEORGIA

Parks, Preserves & Wild Places

Janet Groene
with Gordon Groene

COUNTRY ROADS PRESS
Oaks • Pennsylvania

Natural Wonders of Georgia:
Parks, Preserves & Wild Places

Published by Country Roads Press
P.O. Box 838, 2170 West Drive
Oaks, Pennsylvania 19456

Text design by Studio 3, Ellsworth, Maine.
Illustrations by Lois Leonard Stock.
Typesetting by Typeworks, Belfast, Maine.

ISBN 1-56626-130-9

Library of Congress Cataloging-in-Publication Data

Groene, Janet.
Natural wonders of Georgia : parks, preserves, and wild places / Janet Groene, with Gordon Groene ; illustrator, Lois Leonard Stock.
p. cm.
Includes index.
ISBN 1-56626-130-9
1. Georgia – Guidebooks. 2. Natural history – Georgia – Guidebooks. 3. Natural areas – Georgia – Guidebooks. 4. Parks – Georgia – Guidebooks. 5. Botanical gardens – Georgia – Guidebooks. I. Groene, Gordon. II. Title.
F284.3.G76 1995
917.5804'43 – dc20 95-6032
CIP

Printed in Canada.
10 9 8 7 6 5 4 3 2 1

To the valiant Georgians who endured the Flood of 1994 and to all those in and outside Georgia who gave so selflessly of time, muscle, and money to turn tides of despair to tidings of hope.

And to James Earl Coleman of Fort Gaines, Jack Wingate of Lake Seminole, and the hundreds of other dedicated senior citizens who, with their selfless attention to saving lands and artifacts, are chief among the natural wonders of Georgia.

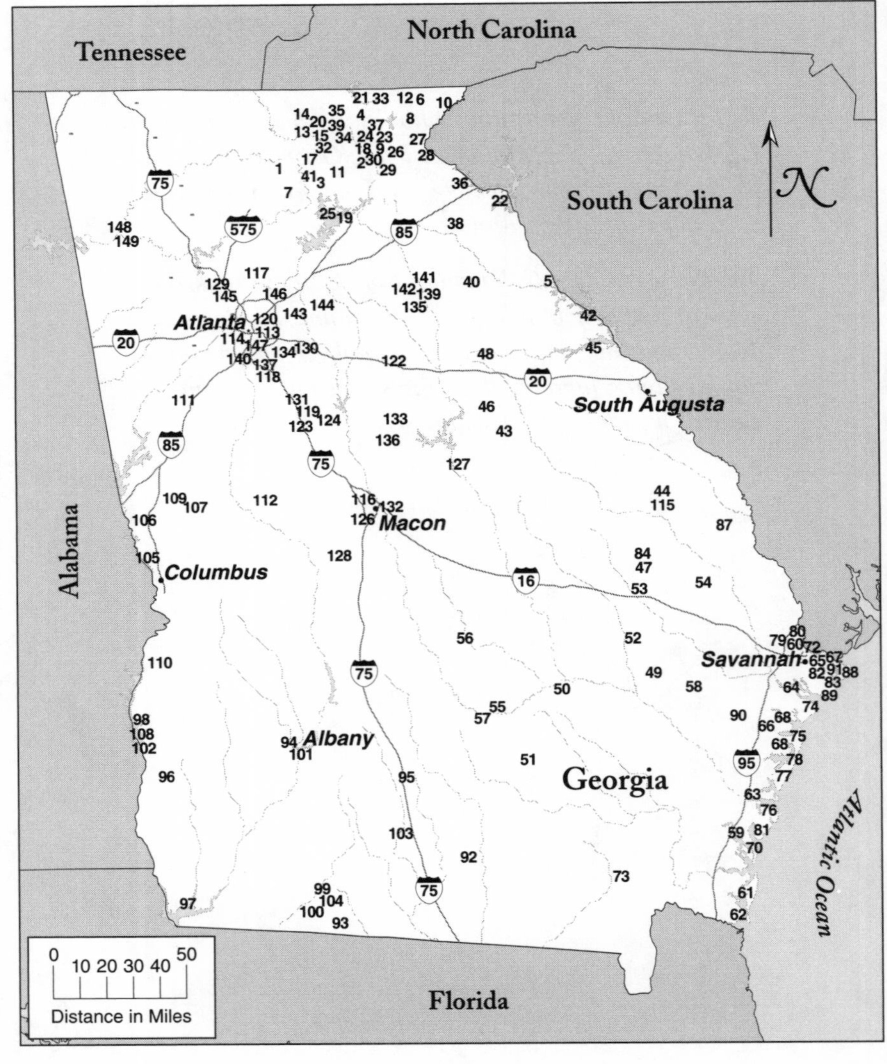

North Carolina
Tennessee
South Carolina
Atlanta
South Augusta
Macon
Columbus
Savannah
Albany
Georgia
Alabama
Atlantic Ocean
Florida
0
10 20 30 40
50
Distance in Miles

Contents

Acknowledgments

Special thanks to Bruce Jewell of the U.S. Forest Service's southern region, Karin P. Koser and Barbara Daniell of the Georgia Division of Tourism and Trade, Becky Morris and her team in the Historic Heartland region, Mary Jo Dudley and her team in the Plantation Trace region, Jenny Stacy of the Savannah Convention and Visitors Bureau, and Paula Pate, formerly of the Thomasville Convention and Visitors Bureau.

Also, Brian Mumma, director of environmental education at Brown's Mount; Bob Lazenby of the Georgia Division of Forestry; Ronnie L. Shell, manager of the Piedmont National Wildlife Refuge; Patsy Pouncey of the Columbus Convention and Visitors Bureau; Phillip and Ramona Kurland of the Dill House in Fort Gaines; Tom Cantrell, who manages Lake Walter F. George Lodge; and Carla Sullivan, interpretive ranger at Panola Mountain State Conservation Park.

Introduction

What scenes pop to mind when you think of Georgia? Do you see the burning of Atlanta in the film *Gone with the Wind*? Presidents, peanuts, the Atlanta Braves? They are as much a part of Georgia as the rusty-red soil itself, but forget them for now and imagine instead the natural wonders of the Peachtree State.

Picture perfumed peach blossoms and magnolias the size of dinner plates. Imagine pecan groves and peanut plantations and fields white with cotton. Forests of pine and oak shelter huge colonies of deer, quail, and wild turkey. Mayhaw grow wild in bogs along creeks that whisper their way through forgotten villages, stranding centuries-old arrowheads on sandbars.

For miles along the Atlantic, brown-sugar beaches bask in steamy sunlight. And the live oaks, bearded with Spanish moss as long as bridal trains, are one of nature's most dramatic sculptures.

Georgia is a vastly varied landscape of flat seacoasts, rolling midlands, and craggy mountains washed by waterfalls.

Its gentle plains, one of America's great farmlands, fall away to the great basin formed by the Chattahoochee River system. Not just a significant river and recreation resource, the Chattahoochee flyway is one of the South's best bird-watching posts. Most wondrous and unique of all the Peachtree State's natural wonders is the sea-sized saucer called the Okefenokee Swamp.

It is no wonder that this natural wonderland is laced with legends, lore, lies, and mysteries, and it is no surprise at all that the people of Georgia's gorgeous outback are so warm and genuine. Southern hospitality here is a cherished tradition, deep as a taproot and sweet as muscadine wine.

We have divided the state into the same sections used by state tourism authorities in their invaluable Official Travel Guide. Titled *Georgia on My Mind*, the magazine-size giveaway is an excellent accompaniment to *Natural Wonders of Georgia* because it tells you about accommodations, dining, additional sightseeing, and practical, nuts-and-bolts information provided by commercial sources.

To get your free copy, call 800-VISIT GA. Then coordinate it, and the state map it contains, with your reading of this book.

The Northeast and Northwest Mountains regions are self-explanatory. Actually the foothills of the Great Smoky Mountains that rise higher as you go northward into North Carolina, these Georgia hills were nevertheless high enough to spawn creeks that once ran bright with the highest-quality gold. The Classic South section is the state's middle east chunk in an arc around Augusta. The Magnolia Midlands spread as far east as the Savannah River; the area's only interstate is I-16, which crosses its northern edges.

South of the Midlands, we carve off the Colonial Coast with its centuries of history, golden marshes, grainy beaches the color of turbinado sugar, and low-lying islands. The southwest corner of the state is called the Plantation Trace region.

It was here that the great cotton plantations thrived during the slave era. Today, the plains here and in the next region north are still a rich breadbasket producing massive harvests of peanuts, canola, soybeans, and other food and forage crops.

The Presidential Pathways Region covers the west central part of the state, which includes President Jimmy Carter's hometown, Plains, as well as President Franklin Roosevelt's vacation home at Warm Springs. Although the state separates Atlanta Metro and the Historic Heartland into two regions, we've described their natural treasures in one combined section.

General Information

State Historic Sites are open 9 A.M. to 5 P.M. Tuesday through Saturday and from 2 to 5:30 P.M. Sunday. Closed Mondays (except legal holidays) and on Thanksgiving and Christmas. Check ahead for special hours at the Little White House and Dahlonega Gold Museum. Small admission charges apply at State Historic Sites; registered guests at state lodges and cottages are admitted free.

State Park admission is a very modest, per-car parking fee. Consider buying the yearly pass even if you're a temporary visitor. Disabled veterans who are Georgia residents get a twenty-five percent discount on campsites, lodge rooms, cottages, swimming, minigolf, greens fees, admissions to historic sites, and annual park passes. (VSO Form 22 is required.)

Senior citizens, age sixty-two and over, get discounts of twenty percent on lodge rooms and cottages during some winter months and on most tent and RV sites all year. The vehicle must be registered to the senior.

State Park hours are from 7 A.M. to 10 P.M. daily except for Panola Mountain, Providence Canyon, and Stephen C. Foster, which vary seasonally. Park offices are generally open daily from 8 A.M. to 5 P.M.

State Farmers' Markets

State farmers' markets, more a meeting place for farmers to sell their produce than tourist attractions, are a natural goal for people who love the bounties of nature. Georgia is first in the United States in the production of peanuts and rye; second in peaches, pecans, poultry, and eggs; and fifth in tomatoes. Open to the public are markets at:

Atlanta, 16 Forest Parkway, 404-366-6910.
Augusta, 1150 Fifth Street, 706-721-3004.
Columbus, 318 Tenth Avenue, 706-649-7448.
Macon, 2055 Eisenhower Parkway, 912-742-8403.
Savannah, 701 US 80 West, 912-966-7800.
Thomasville, 502 Smith Avenue, 912-255-4072.

Nature's Timetable

If you love driving through fragrant farm country, note these dates for Georgia blooms and harvests.

Peaches	Bloom last two weeks in March
Peaches	Fruit late May through mid-August (some varieties mature later.)
Pecans	Bear mid-October to end of December
Wheat	Harvest late May to mid-June
Wheat	Green fields, winter
Cotton	Mid-September to mid-October
Peanut	Harvest mid-September through October

To drive the Peach Blossom Trail, take US 41/19 and State 341 south from Atlanta through Jonesboro, Hampton, Griffin, Barnesville, Culloden, Musella, Roberta, Fort Valley, and Perry, then head back via I-75 with stops in Warner Robins, Forsyth, and McDonough. If you take this route during harvest time, you'll see many roadside stands offering tree-ripened peaches of all varieties and some farms offering pick-your-own peaches.

The Chattahoochee Trace

Eighteen counties in Alabama and Georgia share tourism promotion of the areas east and west of the Chattahoochee River system from West Point Lake south to Lake Seminole and northern Florida. A brochure suggests a number of tours of the area. It is keyed to commercial and historic points of interest, bed and breakfasts, restaurants in historic mansions, and privately owned marinas. Write the Chattahoochee Trail Commission at Box 33, Eufala, AL 36027-0033; 334-687-9755. A natural routing would be to drive up or down the Georgia side and return via the Alabama side.

About Georgia State Forests

Unlike some other states, Georgia does not have an extensive state forest system nor does it have a state forest recreation program. Managed primarily as timber resources, the forests are opened during hunting season and can be explored at other times by motivated visitors who get instructions in advance.

Georgia state forests are the 36,000-acre Dixon Memorial State Forest (4983 Jacksonville Highway, Waycross, GA 31503; 912-287-4915) and the 3,000-acre Baldwin State Forest (1119 Highway 49, Milledgeville, GA 31061; 912-453-5164). The first is a lower-coastal-plain environment growing swamp hardwoods, pine, and cypress. The second, located in the Piedmont, supports mostly loblolly pine and mixed hardwood. Deer, turkeys, squirrels, rabbits, and a wealth of wild birds, abound in both forests. For information, call the state forestry service number below.

The best bet for those who want to explore Georgia's state forest scene is the main office near Macon. Although it's not specifically equipped for visitors and casual dropins are not encouraged because staffers aren't always available to provide tours, there's a small museum, a tree-seed lab, a forest-fire lab, and a center for forest environmental safety. It's on the site of Camp Wheeler, a training site during the two world wars for thousands of troops, many of whom still come by to see the old (but now largely unrecognizable) training grounds.

The Georgia State Forestry Service office is open weekdays from 8 A.M. to 4:30 P.M. Call ahead (912-751-3500) to see if your visit will be appropriate and convenient. From Macon, go east on I-16 to exit 5 and follow signs to the forestry center. No mailing address is published because this office is not equipped to handle mail inquiries.

About Wildlife Management Areas

Hundreds of thousands of Georgia's acres are in wildlife management areas that are opened in specified seasons for managed hunts as well as sometimes for controlled floods or burns.

All are magnificent natural treasures abounding in deer, wild pigs, small game, songbirds, waterfowl, upland birds, amphibians, snakes, butterflies, wildflowers, and flowering shrubs. Some have water frontage and are of interest to boaters, fishermen, and canoeists. Yet these areas are not known to tourism officials and are not described or promoted to tourists. The motivated nature watcher can write to the Game and Fish Division, Department of Natural Resources, 205 Butler Street S.E., Suite 1252 East Towers, Atlanta, GA 30334; 404-918-6400. Ask for the Georgia Hunting Guide, which describes the areas and the hunting laws that apply.

Georgia Film and Video

Through this incredible program, groups and schools can borrow films and videotapes at no charge or purchase them at very modest cost. Titles range from "Talking About

Wood Storks" to "Whitetails: Creatures of the Woods." Subjects are history and natural history. For a catalog, write to Georgia Department of Natural Resources, Film and Video Circulation Manager, 205 Butler Street S.E., Suite 1354, Atlanta, GA 30334.

Georgia's National Forests and Trails

Massive national forests sprawl over central and north Georgia. Both the Chattahoochee National Forest and the Oconee National Forest cover lands in more than one of the tourism divisions in this book. Forest features are discussed individually according to their locations in the Historic Heartland, Classic South, Northwest Mountain, or Northeast Mountain regions.

For maps and descriptions of facilities throughout Oconee and/or Chattahoochee National Forest, write the Forest Supervisor, 508 Oak Street, Gainesville, GA 30501; 404-536-0541. If you're a hiker, request the indispensable Trail Guide, which covers both forests. Dozens of hiking, bicycling, motor biking, horseback riding, and ORV trails are described.

Oconee National Forest covers 109,000 acres, many of them in timber management, mining, wildlife management, cattle grazing, and experimental forestry. Recreation sites also abound. The forest has two campgrounds, four launch ramps, and five fishing lakes. You'll find hiking trails in the Hillsboro Lake, Oconee River, and Lake Sinclair recreation areas; within the park are fifty primitive hunting and fishing camps.

Keep your camera cocked to shoot bald eagles, endangered red-cockaded woodpeckers, large colonies of white-tailed deer, both upland and water birds, and a long list of small mammals as well as a full menu of piedmont trees, wildflowers, and plants.

Chattahoochee National Forest sprawls across almost

the entire northern portion of the state. Choose among nineteen developed recreation areas with four hundred campsites or make camp anywhere in the forest where you don't see a No Camping sign. No permits are required and no fee is charged for primitive camping or picnicking. More than four hundred and thirty miles of trails crisscross the forest, including:

Appalachian Trail: The seventy-nine miles of this historic trail that lie within the Chattahoochee National Forest meet such spots as Springer Mountain and Bly Gap. A separate map is available for a fee. Write to the Appalachian Trail Conference, Box 236, Harpers Ferry, WV. 25425; 304-535-6331.

Bartram Trail: Famous Philadelphia naturalist William Bartram carved a route through Georgia two hundred years ago, naming plants and discovering previously unidentified species, including the Franklinia tree, named for family friend Benjamin Franklin. Now extinct in the wild, the tree survives in private gardens; you can buy seeds at the gift shop at Bartram's Garden, the old family homestead in Philadelphia.

The thirty-seven-mile Bartram Trail starts at the North Carolina state line and continues to the Chattooga River. Near Thomson, at the old village of Wrightsborough, see a church and Quaker cemetery dating to the late eighteenth and early nineteenth centuries. Bartram, who was a Quaker, stayed here in 1773–4.

Duncan Ridge Trail covers thirty-five and a half miles across the Toccoa River, through Fish and Mulky Gaps, and joins the Appalachian Trail after Long Creek.

Benton MacKaye Trail is a fifty-three mile route from Springer Mountain across Skeenah Cap and into the Rich Mountain Wildlife Management Area.

Cohutta Wilderness is a 34,500-acre separate tract of the Chattahoochee National Forest north of Dalton. It is completely surrounded by nonforest lands. Seventy miles of trails give hikers access to remote wilds bordered to the east by the sparkling Conasauga River. Two Georgia highways, State 71 and State 2, also cross the Cohutta.

For further information: Cohutta Ranger District, 401 Old Ellijay Road, Chatsworth, GA 30705; 404-695-6736.

Disclaimer

Even in nature, things change. While this guide is less perishable than books about commercial attractions, natural conditions such as floods or forest fires can cause the closing of a wilderness area. Gardens and zoos may change their hours. Zip codes, telephone numbers, fees, and other features also change in this fast-paced world. Please check ahead before traveling to natural wonders mentioned in these pages.

Georgia Power Recreation Lands

Recreation lands that are managed by Georgia Power are open to the public under certain conditions. Available are 60,000 acres of lakes, 1,350 miles of shoreline, and parks throughout the state with boating, fishing, camping, hiking, tennis, swimming, and other recreational features at fees comparable to those in state parks. Keep in mind that these are privately owned lands. Mailing address: Georgia Power Company, Land Dept., 1516 Barlett's Ferry Road., Fortson 31808.

For information, locations, and operating hours call:
North Georgia/Terrora Park at Tallulah Falls, 404-754-6036
Central Georgia/Lake Oconee, 404-485-8704
South Georgia/Bartletts Ferry, 404-322-0228.

Campsite Definitions

In this book, state park campsites described as tent, RV, or trailer sites have at least some hook-ups, usually water and electricity plus a level pad that may be paved. Other features such as pull-through camping, sewer hook-up, and dump station vary according to individual state parks.

In Georgia state parks, walk-in campsites do not have water, electricity, or garbage containers but usually do have a picnic table, fire ring, and access to a comfort station. Campers must walk to the tent pad from the parking area. Primitive campsites are accessed by trail only, and have no water spigot (although other water may be available), electricity, or toilet. Pioneer camping is for groups only.

1

Northeast Mountains

Only an hour north of Atlanta's skyscrapers and humming traffic, you're suddenly in a rugged wilderness that is upholstered in mountain forests and laced with waterfalls formed by sparkling trout streams. Winters are cold enough to provide snow skiing; at high altitudes, summers days are sunny and fresh while nights are pleasantly cool.

In spring, mountain laurels and azaleas put on an extravagant show, soon followed by the poetry of pink and white rhododendrons. Tramp forest trails to browse a catalog of wildflowers: wild ginger, chickweed, the pink clusters of bouncing Bet, fleshy sedum, and the showy blooms of Saint-John's-wort. In autumn, changing leaves paint the hills with a bright brush as sumac, sourwood, hardwoods, and dogwood change into winter coats.

In the lowlands, look for tufted titmice nesting in old woodpecker holes and venturing out to dine on sumac, bayberry, and yellow poplar. Boggy spruce woods are home to rusty blackbirds while weedy fields invite communities of brilliant goldfinches. Lakes mean a colorful blend of ducks;

highlands host hawks, bald eagles, and the occasional peregrine falcon nesting in a high cliff.

Runaway rivers have been dammed to create placid lakes with rambling shorelines and wooded islands while old villages have attracted writers, artists, and crafters who celebrate nature's themes. Many of the most scenic overlooks and leafy forests have been lightly developed with chalet communities or state-owned lodges. For the latter, reserve early; they're very popular all year.

It all began with the discovery of the region's most precious natural wonder: gold. The forty-niners rushed west to the Yukon, not realizing that the mountains of Georgia were already yielding some of the purest gold in the world. So much of the precious metal was lost during primitive mining attempts, it is said that there is still enough gold in them thar hills to pave the town square a foot deep.

Local centers throughout the area invite visitors to pan for gold and/or mine gemstones. It's exciting outdoor fun, and everyone has a story about the tourist who made the Big Strike.

Come to northeast Georgia to rest in a rustic cabin overlooking a great view or to pursue the most rugged sports, including white-water rafting, rock climbing, cross-country or downhill skiing, and backpacking; or to go trout fishing.

Observe safety rules. Check in with rangers for current advice, don't attempt to climb waterfalls, and don't drink the water (unless labeled safe). Giardiasis is a threat.

The Appalachian Trail in Georgia winds for seventy-nine scenic miles between Springer Mountain and Bly Gap. A guidebook to the trail can be ordered for a fee from Appalachian Trail Conference, Box 236, Harpers Ferry WV 25425; 304-5356331. The most famous of the state's trails, it's also the most crowded, so don't overlook the area's many other long and scenic trails.

Amicola Falls State Park

This 729-foot waterfall, the highest east of the Rockies, provides a dramatic setting for the approach to Georgia's segment of the Appalachian Trail. An eight-mile trail connects the two.

A fifty-seven-room lodge with stunning mountain views makes roughing it easy, and the lodge's Maple Restaurant serves up hearty fare at modest prices. A more rustic, walk-in lodge, opened in 1993, has proved immensely popular.

Sit on a rocker to watch soaring raptors catch updrafts or hike three and a half miles of rugged trails through the mountains and to myriad waterfalls. Throughout the summer, rangers lead nature programs and, in October, there's an organized backpacking trip at the height of autumn color.

Where: Fifteen miles northwest of Dawsonville. Take State 53 West from Dawsonville, then State 183 to State 52 East.
Facilities: Lodges, hiking and nature trails, picnic area with shelters, restaurant, tent and RV camping, trout fishing.
For more information: Amicola Falls State Park, Star Route, Box 215, Dawsonville, GA 30534; 706-265-8888.

Anna Ruby Falls Scenic Area

Where Curtis Creek drops 1,534 feet and York Creek fifty feet, waters thunder together to form Anna Ruby Falls. Twin curtains of water drop down the stark cliff face, then cascade over rocks and become rushing creeks on their way to the Apalachicola River and, finally, the Gulf of Mexico. The falls were named for Anna Ruby Nichols, daughter of a Confederate veteran who purchased the falls and surrounding land. After Captain Nichols died in 1898, the area was logged out, but it came under national protection in 1925 and has regained its natural loveliness.

Under majestic white pine and noble poplar, look for

bird's-foot violets, sessile trilliums, and foam flowers. Large areas are carpeted with fern and moss. Streams sparkle with brook trout under canopies of oak and hemlock. In springtime, mountain laurel and rhododendron bloom.

Hike the paved, half-mile footpath from the parking lot or the more challenging and rewarding four-and-six-tenths-mile Smith Creek Trail from Unicoi State Park to the falls. Squirrel and wild turkeys are commonly seen. Deer and bear are also here, but are spotted only by the persistent and lucky.

Where: Take State 75 northeast from Helen for a mile to Robertstown, then go northeast (right) on State 356 for one and a half miles, then turn left at the falls entrance and go three and six-tenths miles to the parking area. The walk to the base of the falls is paved, but can be wet and slippery. A parking fee is charged.
For more information: Chattooga Ranger District, Burton Road. Highway. 197, Charlesville, GA 30523; 404-754-6221.
Facilities: Craft shop with restrooms. Two trails, one accessible to people with mobility or sight impairments.

Antique Rose Emporium

Georgia's mansions are filled with original furnishings dating back two and three centuries, so it seems only natural that the state has also found a home for antique roses that are actual descendants of plants introduced centuries ago in the Americas, Europe, and the Orient. The Cherokee rose, a native of China, does so well here it is the state flower. Another, Champneys Pink Cluster is believed to be the first rose known to have been bred in America. It was the first of the now-classic Noisette class.

The Antique Rose Emporium outside Dahlonega is primarily a nursery and catalog house, but visitors are also welcome to walk paths of roses, shrubs, and herbs under canopies of native rhododendron, ferns, dogwoods, and oaks along the Chestatee River. Profusions of roses are a gardener's delight: tree roses, bushes, ramblers, climbers, container-grown miniatures, and the most fragrant long-stems.

Roses that once made up a nosegay for a Victorian lady or graced the gardens of Empress Josephine or rambled heedlessly along old farm fences, have been saved here by dedicated naturalists who call themselves rose rustlers. When they see a forgotten rose in an old community or along a country road, they take a cutting and propagate it. Dozens of old roses have been saved this way. The Emporium's eighty-page catalog, which sells for $5, is one of the state's best souvenir buys as well as a working catalog from which visitors can order roses for their own dooryards.

Where: North two and a half miles on State 52 from Dahlonega, then right on Cavender's Creek Road for five miles. Look for the Emporium a half mile after passing Copper Mines Road.
For more information: Route 1, Box 630, Dahlonega, GA 30533; 706-846-5884. Hours vary. Call ahead.
Facilities: Gift shop, nursery, gardens, restrooms.

Brasstown Bald

At 4,784 feet, Brasstown Bald is the highest mountain in Georgia. The three-hundred-and-sixty-degree view is well worth climbing the steep, half-mile trail. Or take the shuttle bus from the parking lot to the summit.

Where: Take US 19 and 129 south from Blairsville for eight miles, then go east (left) on State 180 for nine miles and north (left) on the State 180 spur three more miles.
Facilities: Picnicking, gift shop, visitors center open seasonally, restrooms.

For more information: Brasstown Ranger District, P.O. Box 9, Blairsville, GA 30512; 706-745-6928. Fees for parking, shuttle.

Bobby Brown State Park

During the 1790s, a bustling village stood here, but today the place where the Broad and Savannah Rivers flow into Clark Hill Reservoir is a wooded playground around a 78,000-acre lake. The waters are popular with anglers, boaters, and water-skiers; swimmers may prefer the pool. Leave the crowds behind by climbing the two-mile trail to a perch that overlooks the lake into lands that were once covered with vast plantations.

Where: Twenty-one miles southeast of Elberton off State 72 on Bobby Brown Park Road.
Facilities: Tent and trailer campsites, pool, snack bar, boat ramp and dock, picnic shelters, fishing, boating.
For more information: Bobby Brown State Park, Route 4, Box 232, Elberton, GA 30635; 706-213-2046.

Black Rock Mountain State Park

Sitting astride the eastern Continental Divide, this portion of the Appalachians forms the highest state park in Georgia. Toil high on the trails for breathtaking views of the Appalachians, especially the dark granite "black" cliffs that gave this park its name. Not far away, the Chattooga River offers some of the best white-water rafting in the East while Sky Valley is one of the Southeast's premier ski areas.

Where: Three miles north of Clayton via US 441.
Facilities: Tent and trailer camping, rental cottages, lake, picnic shelters, mountain culture programs, three hiking trails.
For more information: Black Rock Mountain State Park, Mountain City, GA 30562; 706-746-2141.

Burt's Pumpkin Farm

Pumpkins of every size and shape are a lantern carver's delight and a pie maker's dream. Surrounded by the mountains' natural wonders is this wholesome, down-home fun farm where visitors can take a tractor hayride and watch popcorn being processed in season.

Where: On State 183, fifteen miles northwest of Dawsonville, GA; 706-265-3701.
For more information: Chamber of Commerce, Courthouse, Public Square, Dawsonville, GA 30545.

Chattahoochee National Forest

The entire northeast corner of Georgia lies within the Chattahoochee National Forest, and most of the recreation sites are here. However, the main forest and two smaller tracts that are not contiguous to it extend into the northwest section of the state. See other sections for additional Chattahoochee National Forest listings. Points of interest are listed separately in their own regions.

For information and maps: Write to the Forest Ranger, U.S. Forest Service, 508 Oak Street N.W., Gainesville, GA 30501.

Chattahoochee River Recreation Area

The mighty Chattahoochee River threads through the entire state and is surrounded by recreation lands. Here you'll explore the headwaters of the river and Horse Trough Falls in the rugged Mark Trail Wilderness Area.

Where: Take Georgia 75 north from Helen for one and a half miles, then go left on Georgia 356 (Alternate 75) across the river, then right on the paved road next to the Chattahoochee

Church. The pavement ends, but follow the road nine miles more to the campground.
Facilities: Camping, picnicking, flush toilets, hiking trails, drinking water.
For more information: U.S. Forest Service, 508 Oak Street, Gainesville GA 30501; 706-536-0541.

Chattooga River

This crashing white-water stream was famed and defamed in the film *Deliverance*, and is usually associated more with North Carolina than with Georgia, but it does flow into the Peachtree State. For rafting reservations, call the Nantahala Outdoor Center, 800-232-7238 or 704-488-2175. For information about Georgia lodgings in the river region, contact Rabun County Tourism, Box 750, Clayton, GA 30525; 706-782-4812.

Chestatee River

Once the boundary of Cherokee territory before frenzied gold seekers wrested the land away from the tribe and marched the Indians west to Oklahoma, the Chestatee River is today a creamy cauldron of whitewater studded with white sand strands where tubers, canoers, and kayakers can stop for a sunbath or a picnic.

Outfitters uncomplicate things by providing gear, shuttle trips, and wilderness-wise guides. Sign on for any of nine trips lasting from two to ten hours through Class I and II rapids, past stands of rhododendron, towering cliffs, and fragrant hemlock forests. Overnight canoe-camping trips are also offered.

Facilities: Shuttle service, gear rental, canoe clinics. Prepare to get wet and muddy in backwoods conditions with no facilities.
For more information: Appalachian Outfitters, Box 793,

Highway 60 South, Dahlonega, GA 30533; 706-864-7117 or 800-426-7117.

Coleman River Wildlife Management Area

Managed primarily for the wildlife, which is thinned out in yearly hunts, this 11,000-acre tract is also ideal for nature watching, primitive camping, and fishing.

Where: Go west eight miles from Clayton to Tallulah River Road, then right for four and a half miles to Coleman River Road, then left half a mile to the check-in station.
For more information: Rabun Convention and Visitors Bureau, Box 750, Clayton, GA 30525; 706-782-4812 or Department of Natural Resources, 205 Butler Street S.E., Suite 1252, East Towers, Atlanta, GA 30334; 404-918-6400.

Cooper's Creek Wildlife Management Area

Hunt these 34,000 wilderness acres in the heart of the Chattahoochee National Forest or just camp out and enjoy the piney silence or the rushing creeks where white-tailed deer come to drink or the rugged mountain hiking.

Where: Take US 19 north from Dahlonega to State 60, then go north seventeen miles to U.S. Forest Service Road 236, then right to the check-in station.
Facilities: Primitive camping.
For more information: Department of Natural Resources, 205 Butler Street S.E., Suite 1252, East Towers, Atlanta, GA 30334; 404-918-6400.

Cooper's Creek Scenic and Recreation Area

Another 1,240-acre tract has been set aside here along Cooper's Creek and its tributaries, allowing easier access to this wilderness and its legendary trout fishing.

Where: From Blairsville, go west on US 76 for three miles, then left on Mulky Gap Road. When the pavement ends, go three miles more to find Cooper's Creek on your left.
Facilities: Picnicking, tent and RV camping, hiking trails, fishing, restrooms, drinking water.
For more information: Chamber of Commerce, 385 Blue Ridge Highway, Blairsville, GA 30512; 706-745-5789.

Coosa Bald

This 7,100-acre parcel in the Chattahoochee National Forest looks like a giant's playground, strewn with huge Pleistocene-era boulders that were left stranded by the last retreating glacier. Among them grow a rich diversity of rare plants, many of them introduced eons ago by glacial crawl and found nowhere else in the state.

You'll see deer, raccoons, opossums, and perhaps a black bear, as well as a three-act opera of songbirds and plenty of raptors.

Where: Take US 19 and 129 south from Blairsville for ten miles, then go west (right) on Georgia 180 for another seven miles. Mailing address: Brasstown Ranger District, P.O. Box 9, Blairsville, GA 30512; 706-745-6928.
Facilities: None.

Crisson and Consolidated Gold Mines

At the family-owned Crisson Gold Mine, which goes back to 1847, visitors are welcome to pan for gold and gems. Learn the art of gold panning, make some new friends, and enjoy the sweet mountain air.

Where: On Wimpy Mill Road, off State 19 North, two and a half miles from downtown Dahlonega. Open every day from

Black bear

10 A.M., closing at 6 P.M. June through August and 5 P.M. other months. Admission.

Facilities: Camping (706-864-7017), gift shop selling gold nuggets and handmade gold jewelry. Gold panning also at nearby Blackburn Park, south of Dahlonega on Auraria Road, formerly State 9E. This park also offers an archery range, camping, swimming, fishing, and mountain hiking. Open daily 7 A.M. to 10 P.M.; 864-3711 or 864-4050.

Also pan for gold at Consolidated Mines, a mile east of Dahlonega on Georgia 19 and 60 N. Connector. Mines here closed in the 1930s, but many a nugget has yet to be found. It's the largest mining operation east of the Mississippi and plant tours are offered. Call 706-864-3711 or 864-8473.

For more information: Crisson Gold Mine, Route 5, Box 807, Dahlonega, GA 30533; 706-864-6363.

DeSoto Falls Scenic Area

Wade in clear streams, hike at elevations as high as 3,400 feet, and picnic at overlooks that seem to drop off to nowhere. This 650-acre park is threaded with sparkling streams and waterfalls.

Where: Take US 19 north from Dahlonega for thirteen and a half miles, then turn left at Turner's Corner onto US 129, then four and two-tenths miles. 706-864-3711.

Facilities: Picnicking, camping and showers, hiking trails, drinking water, restrooms.

For more information: Chamber of Commerce, 101 South Park Street, Dahlonega, GA 30533. Or Chestatee District Ranger, 1015 Tipton Drive, Dahlonega, GA 30533; 706-864-6173.

Dukes Creek Falls Trail

A driving tour of this area is described below, but don't miss the chance to scramble up and down this steep, rugged, eight-tenths of a mile dirt-and-gravel switchback trail. It takes you into a gorge right across from the falls. Caution: don't leave the designated trail and don't climb the falls.

Where: Take State 75 north from Helen for one and a half miles, then go left on State 356/Alternate 75. At the bridge,

go left two and two-tenths miles to Forest Service Road 348 (Richard Russell Scenic Highway). Turn right, then 2 miles to the Dukes Creek parking area.
Facilities: None.
For more information: Forest Service Supervisor, 601 Broad Street, Gainesville, GA 30501; 770-536-0541.

Elachee Nature Center

This Gainesville nature preserve covers 1,200 steeply contoured acres. At its core is a nature center encompassing botanical gardens, exhibits, trails, and a museum. Call in advance to ask about special programs that will acquaint you with the old and new ecology of an area that has been transformed in this century by the addition of dams and sprawling lakes.

Where: On Old Atlanta Highway, Gainesville; 770-535-1976.
Facilities: Exhibits, natural history museum, arts and crafts, programs, marked trails, restrooms, picnic tables. Nature center open daily 10 A.M. to 4 P.M. Sunday 2 to 4 P.M.
For more information: Convention and Visitors Bureau, 830 Green Street, Gainesville, GA 30501; 770-536-5209.

Frank Gross Recreation Area

A fishing and camping paradise has been set aside on the most scenic section of Rock Creek near the Chattahoochee National Fish Hatchery. Take State 60 north from Suches about ten miles, then go left on Forest Service Road 69 for five miles.
For more information: Chamber of Commerce, 385 Blue Ridge Highway, Blairsville, GA 30512; 706-745-5789.

Fred Hamilton Rhododendron Garden

More than 2,000 rhododendrons and azaleas frame fields of wildflowers. Peak seasons for various blooms vary.

Where: Georgia Mountain Fairgrounds, US 76 West, Hiwassee.
Facilities: Restrooms, extensive entertainment, and crafts exhibits during the fair in August and October.
For more information: Georgia Mountain Fair Inc., Box 444, Hiwassee, GA 30546; 706-896-4191.

Hartwell Lake

The state park that surrounds this 56,000-acre reservoir covers only 146 acres, so it's the lake itself—nestled in the steep, wooded hills—that is the appeal here. It's popular with fisherfolk and water-skiers, but there are always quiet coves around the shoreline where nature's ad-lib show continues for the patient observer.

Deer come to drink at dawn and dusk, and raccoons might be spotted wetting down the day's dinner in the shallows. Look for sparrows in the thickets, the occasional fox or bear, goldfinches in weedy fields, and cliff swallows on their way to South America for the winter.

Where: Go East from Hartwell on US 29, then go left on Ridge Road two miles to the state park.
Facilities: Campsites, cottages, swimming beach, picnic shelters, boat launch, music programs.
For more information: Hart State Park, 1515 Hart Park Road, Hartwell, GA 30643; 706-376-8756.

High Shoals Scenic Area

Take the one-mile trail along splashing mountain streams, walking on banks that are lined with rhododendron and laurel. You'll see two waterfalls and a world of wildlife.

Where: Take State 75 north from Cleveland for twenty-two miles, then go east (right) on Forest Service Road 283 for a mile to the trailhead to Blue Hole Falls. 706-745-6928.

Facilities: None.
For more information: Forest Service, 508 Oak Street, Gainesville, GA 30501; 770-536-0541.

Horse Trough Falls Trail

Even if you're not a hero hiker, try tackling this trail because it is less than half a mile long and not too steep. The winding path takes you through a sweetly serene forest, across mountain streams on slippery stepping stones, and to the base of this picture-postcard waterfall.

Where: Take State 74 north eight miles from Helen to Unicoi Gap, then go left on Forest Service Road 44 (Wilkes Creek Road) for five and a half miles. At the curve, take the right fork, then two-tenths of a mile to a one-lane wooden bridge. From here, blue blazes show you the way to the trail.

An alternate route is to take State 74 north one and a half miles to State 356. Turn left at the bridge, crossing the Chattahoochee River, then go one-tenth of a mile to the first right (Forest Service Road 52), then eight and a half miles to Forest Service Road 44. Turn left and go for two-tenths of a mile, cross the wooden bridge, and look for the blue blazes.
Facilities: None.
For more information: Forest Service Supervisor, 508 Oak Street, Gainesville, GA 30501; 770-536-0541.

Lake Lanier Islands

Nature needed help in creating this massive, meandering lake and its sprinkling of softly wooded islands, but it has been many years since the initial damming and rechanneling of the Chattahoochee River, and today this 1,200-acre state playland can be claimed as a natural wonder.

There's plenty of sporty razzmatazz, including superb Hilton and Stouffer resorts, but the nature lover can still find a secluded campsite, miles of unpeopled shoreline, uninhabited islets rimmed with pebbled beaches, and uncrowded walking paths.

Where: Access is from Buford and Gainesville.
Facilities: Golf course, resorts, snacking and fine dining, camping, horseback riding, boat rental, beaches, water park, entertainment. The Lake Lanier Museum of Natural History is at 2601 Buford Dam Road, Buford; 404-932-4460. Incorporated in the museum is a 150-foot observation tower with an excellent view of the lake and countryside. Free. Hours vary seasonally. Phone first.
For more information: Lake Lanier Islands, 6950 Holiday Road, Lake Lanier, GA 30518; 770-932-7200. Admission, fees.

Moccasin Creek State Park

Cradled by the Blue Ridge Mountains and edged by the Appalachian Trail, this tiny 32-acre park within the Chattahoochee National Forest is a breeding ground for trout, which must have the kind of clear, clean water that flows here. Senior citizens and children under age twelve, may fish in the stream, and there's also a wheelchair-accessible fishing pier.

Launch a boat on Lake Burton or just hike the bouldery creek banks to be lulled by the song of the waters. The park is a favorite jumping-off point for rafting the Chattooga River or visiting Tallulah Gorge.

Where: Twenty miles north of Clarkesville on State 197.
Facilities: Tent and trailer sites, playground, boat docks and ramp, wheelchair-accessible fishing, picnic area, trout-rearing station tours, two-mile hiking trail plus nearby Appalachian Trail.
For more information: Moccasin Creek State Park, Route 1, Box 1634, Clarkesville, GA 30523; 706-947-3194.

Additional information: For white-water rafting reservations, Nantahala Outdoor Center, Box 1390, Clayton, GA 30525; 800-232-7238; or Southeastern Expeditions, Highway 76, Clayton, GA 30525; 800-868-RAFT. For area hiking, canoe, kayaking, and horseback-riding information, write the Rabun County Convention and Visitors Bureau, Box 750, Clayton, GA 30525; welcome center is on US 441 North, Clayton; 706-7824812. For snow skiing, contact Sky Valley Skiing, Sky Valley, GA 30537; 706-746-5302. Kayaking day trips on lakes in the area are available through Shoo Cow Kayak Co.; 706-754-5885.

The check-in station for Lake Burton Wildlife Management Area, a 13,000-acre portion of Chattahoochee National Forest that is open seasonally to hunters, is twenty one miles north of Clayton on State 197. The check-in station is the Lake Burton Fish Hatchery. Mailing address: Department of Natural Resources, 2198 Northlake Parkway, Building 10, Suite 108, Tucker, GA 30084; 404-414-3333.

Tallulah Falls and Gorge

When you look down into this awesome chasm, imagine Karl Wallenda walking across it on a tightrope. That's one of the modern claims to fame of this ancient area, which is said to be the oldest natural gorge in the United States. At 1,100 feet deep, it is second only to the Grand Canyon in depth.

Hike a 2,200-foot trail around the rim of the gorge, where you'll also see Hurricane, Tempesta, and Oceana Falls. Then amble the nature walk at a leisurely pace to make note of the names of trees and other features. A gallery sells the work of local painters, potters, weavers, and other crafters.

Where: Terrora Visitors Center is on US 41.

Facilities: Camping, hiking, restrooms and food service at various spots, gift shops, museum, nature walks, exhibits and interactive video at the visitors center.

For more information: Terrora Visitors Center, Box 9, Tallulah Falls, GA 30573; 706-754-3276. Terrora Park, which has trails, picnic grounds, swimming, camping, and a playground overlooking Tallulah Falls, is on US 441/23.

Toccoa Falls

A hydroelectric plant here that once supplied the town with electricity has been restored as a historic attraction.

Where: On State 17 North in Toccoa.

Facilities: Gift shops, restaurant. Travelers Rest Historic Site nearby is a restored nineteenth-century stagecoach inn with original furnishings, 706-886-2256. Admission. Also downtown in Toccoa is the twenty-five-acre Henderson Falls Park with playgrounds, tennis courts, picnic tables, and nature trails to the waterfall. See Main Street Toccoa address below.

For more information: Main Street Toccoa, Box 579, Toccoa, GA 30577; 706-886-8451.

Mount Yonah

It's rugged going, but you can drive almost to the top of this 3,100-foot mountain on a forest service road. The mountain's slick rock face is used by the U.S. Army for rappelling training. Some of the land is government owned and some is in private hands, so don't leave the road. There are no marked public areas.

Where: Look for the service road off State 75 between Cleveland and Helen.

Facilities: None.

For more information: Forest Service Supervisor, 601 Broad Street, Gainesville, GA 30501; 770-536-0541. Order topographical maps (fee) from Georgia Geological Survey, 19 Martin Luther King, Jr. Drive, Atlanta, GA 30334; 404-656-3214.

Raven Cliff Falls

Take a taxing two-hour walk, climbing steep grades and fording streams through a land of rippling waterfalls and chuckling cascades to end up at the base of stunning Raven Cliff Falls. Don't stray from the marked trail and be very cautious, especially when crossing the rock bluff.

Where: Take State 75 north one and a half miles from Helen, then go left at the bridge onto Alternate 75/State 356 and proceed two and two-tenths miles to the Richard Russell Scenic Highway. Turn right, go two and eight-tenths miles, and look for the parking area on the road at the trail head.
Facilities: Primitive campsites, picnic area.
For more information: Forest Service Supervisor, 601 Broad Street, Gainesville, GA 30501; 770-536-0541.

Richard B. Russell State Park

The site dates back to Paleo Indians ten thousand years ago, but today this 2,700-acre state park is one of the state's newest. It's manicured more for recreation than for communing with nature, but that also means good wheelchair access at all its facilities. The park's most popular feature is a 26,500-acre lake that roars with boating and waterskiing activity. For a quieter experience, take to the hiking trails.

Where: Nine miles northeast of Elberton off State 77 on Ruckersville Road.
Facilities: Beach, concessions, docks and boat ramp, picnic shelters, lake, hiking paths.

For more information: Richard B. Russell State Park, Route 2, Box 118, Elberton, GA 30635; 706-213-2045.

Sosebee Cove Scenic Area

Said to be one of the best stands of second-growth yellow poplars in the nation, this 175-acre forest tract is peppered with wildflowers. It's a memorial to Arthur Woody, the "barefoot" ranger who served in this area from 1911 to 1945.

Where: Take US 19/129 south from Blairsville for ten miles, then go west (right) on Georgia 180 for two miles.
Facilities: None except for a half-mile trail.
For more information: Brasstown Ranger District, P.O. Box 9, Blairsville, GA 30512; 706-745-6928.

Tallulah River

Less well known than the popular Tallulah Falls, this area farther north on the Tallulah River is set in craggy hills where wildlife and humans alike have come for many years to find rich harvests of trout in clear, clean streams.

Where: Take US 76 west from Clayton for eight miles, then go north (right) on a paved, unnumbered country road for four miles, then northwest (left) on Forest Service Road 70 for a mile.
Facilities: Camping, hiking, flush toilets, drinking water. Also on US 76, twelve miles west of Clayton, is an interesting experiment in recycling. Popcorn Overlook is a picnic site furnished with tables, benches, and other facilities made from recycled plastic and wood fiber. No restrooms.
For more information: Tallulah Ranger District, 825 Highway 441 South, P.O. Box 438, Clayton, GA 30525; 706-782-3320.

Russell-Brasstown Scenic Byway

Because this is a driving tour, it is a must-do for people who are mobility impaired. The spectacular loop tour stops at overlooks and interpretive signs where visitors can gaze out over the mountains and piedmont. The route passes Dukes Creek Falls, which plunges a spectacular three hundred feet into a chasm. Hike the mile-long trail here, stopping at observation points, picnic sites, and the craft shop.

Where: Go north on State 17/75 from Helen, then west (left) on State 180, south (left) on State 348, and east (left) on Alternate State 75 back to Helen. 706-745-6928.
For more information: Chattooga Ranger District, Box 196, Burton Road, Clarkesville, GA 30523; 706-754-6221.

Trackrock Archaeological Area

Centuries ago, unknown Indians carved human footprints, bird tracks, animals, circles, and crosses into the rocks here.

Where: Take US 19/129 south from Blairsville, then go east on County 95 Town Creek Road for five miles.
Facilities: None.
For more information: Chamber of Commerce, 385 Blue Ridge Highway, Blairsville, GA 30512; 706-745-5789.

Tugaloo State Park

Nature's scheme of things here has been disturbed in modern times with the damming of the Tugaloo River and the creation of Hartwell Reservoir, which surrounds this 393-acre state park. Although the forest is young, it's already sweetly scattered with wildflowers and atwitter with bird life. This is a highly developed park, popular with weekenders, but follow the nature trails for quiet strolls away from the crowds.

Where: North of Lavonia, off State 328.
Facilities: Tent and trailer camping, cottages, tennis, trails, beach and bathhouse, miniature golf, boat ramps, good bass fishery.
For more information: Tugaloo State Park, Route 1, Box 1766, Lavonia, GA 30553; 706-3564362.

Unicoi State Park

This forested, 1,081-acre park nestles on wooded hills around a fifty-three-acre lake not far from Georgia's highest mountain, Brasstown Bald. Hike twelve miles of rugged trails through pines, mountain laurel, and towering rhododendrons.

Where: Two miles northeast of Helen on State 356.
Facilities: Cottages, campsites, swimming beach, hiking trails, mountain-culture programs, craft shop, primitive (walk-in) camping, boating, fishing, one-hundred-room lodge with buffet dining.
For more information: Unicoi State Park, Box 849, Helen, GA 30545; 706-8782201. Reservations, 706-878-2824.

Victoria Bryant State Park

The mountains here in Georgia's upper piedmont have softened into rolling hills that offer easy hiking on five miles of trails through oaks, maples, and other hardwoods. Keep your binoculars handy for sightings of grouse, wild turkey, woodpecker, and owl. In early summer, seek out such wildflowers as Dutchman's-pipe and wild ginger. Look for the white blooms of toadflax on the roots of oak trees and along the roadsides the blooms of blue-weed, which turn pink with age.

Where: Two miles north of Franklin Springs on State 327.

Facilities: Golf course, tent and trailer camping, playgrounds, swimming pool, picnic shelters, hiking trails, stocked fish pond.
For more information: Victoria Bryant State Park, Route 1, Box 1767, Royston, GA 30662; 706-245-6270.

Vogel State Park

Getting here is half the fun. Driving to this 280-acre park from the south, you'll pass through Neel's Gap, a scenic mountain pass near the highest point in Georgia, 4,784-foot high Brasstown Bald. Come in springtime to see mountain laurel, in early summer to delight in rhododendron, in fall for the electric reds and yellows as leaves change.

Although the park can be touristy in season, you can escape the crowds on seventeen miles of hiking trails, including access to the Appalachian Trail.

Where: Off US 19/129 between Dahlonega and Blairsville.
Facilities: Miniature golf, lake, beach, bathhouse, picnic shelters, tent and trailer campsites, pedal boat rental, rental cottages, mountain music programs.
For more information: Vogel State Park, Route 1, Box 1230, Blairsville, GA 30512; 706-745-2628.

Watson Mill Bridge State Park

Although it's best known for its man-made wonder, the longest wooden bridge still on its original site in Georgia, this pretty, 144-acre park also encompasses thickly forested lands and a mirror-flat millpond. It's a favorite hideaway for picnickers, campers, canoeists, and fishermen. Try for bass, catfish, and bream in the pond behind the old dam. In summer and at Christmas, come for the outdoor concerts. Photograph the 229-foot-long, wood-pegged bridge; walk the easy nature trails.

GEORGIA'S WINERIES

Two vineyards and wineries are in Georgia's northeast mountains at Braselton. Both offer tours of manicured grounds, gardens, and vineyards, as well as tours of the winemaking, with wine tastings. Chateau Elan is a resort with spa, restaurant, and lodge. Chestnut Mountain is known for its lawns and rose gardens as well as its vineyards.

Where: **Chateau Elan and Chestnut Mountain Winery are both at exit 48 off I-85.**

For more information: **Chateau Elan, 7000 Old Winder Highway, Braselton, GA 30517; 770-932-0900. Chestnut Mountain Winery, Braselton, GA 30517; 770-867-6914.**

Where: Three miles southeast of Comer off State 22.
Facilities: Canoe and pedal-boat rental, restrooms, picnic shelters, tent and trailer campsites, fishing, interpretive site at the old grist-mill.
For more information: Watson Bill Bridge State Park, Route 1, Box 190, Comer, GA 30629; 706-783-5349. State park fees apply.

Woody Gap

This is the point where the Appalachian Trail crosses State 60, so it's a good spot from which to have a tentative look at the trail as well as a view of the Yahoola Valley.

Where: Go north on State 60 from Dahlonega for fourteen miles.
Facilities: Picnicking, hiking, flush toilets.
For more information: Forest Ranger, Box 9, Blairsville, GA 30512; 706-745-6928.

2

Classic South

Bordered to the east by South Carolina and the Savannah River, and to the west by Lake Oconee, this region welcomes visitors who are arriving via I-20 with a pleasant Welcome Center at Martinez. Augusta is this region's chief city; Lake Oconee and Clark Hill Lake are its biggest reservoirs.

It's a friendly, uncrowded wedge of the state, far from the city seductions of Atlanta and Savannah. Driving I-20 near Thomson between exits 59 and 60, keep an eye out for herds of unusual black-and-white cows called Belted Galloway. They look like Oreo cookies-on-the-hoof.

Elijah Clark State Park

Clark Hill Lake, an enormous reservoir formed when the Savannah River was dammed, is a major recreational resource with miles of wooded and wetland shoreline and countless parks and access points. If you want to rent one of the cozy cottages here, reserve well in advance.

Where: Seven miles north of Lincolnton off US 378.

Facilities: Tent and trailer camping, boat launch, museum (open weekends), miniature golf, picnicking, water skiing, trails.
For more information: Elijah Clark State Park, Route 4 Box 293, Lincolnton, GA 30827; 706-359-3458.

Note: Also see Mistletoe State Park section. Primitive camping and public access on the lake are also available through the Clark Hill Lake Wildlife Management Area, where hunting is permitted in season. The 15,000-acre wilderness is managed by the U.S. Army Corps of Engineers, 77 Forsyth Street, S.W., Room 313, Atlanta, GA 30335; 404-331-6746.
Where: From exit 50 on I-20 take US 78 north ten miles, then right on the dirt road at the Georgia Department of Natural Resources sign and two and a half miles to the check-in.
Facilities: Primitive camping.
For more information: Department of Natural Resources, 205 Butler Street S.E., Suite 1252, East Towers, Atlanta, GA 30334; 404-918-6400.

Hamburg State Park

The Little Ogeechee River still flows through this site, where it has been powering a gristmill since the 1920s. Rent a canoe to paddle the cool waters, then stop by the mill to buy freshly ground cornmeal to make pone for dinner. The impoundment is open for boating and fishing all year; the Ogeechee is best for canoeing in March and April.

Where: Six miles northeast of Warthen via Hamburg Road off State 102.
Facilities: Tent and trailer sites, stocked fishing lake, boat rentals, educational programs, museum, picnic shelters, gristmill, country store.

For more information: Hamburg State Park, Route 1, Box 233, Mitchell, GA 30820; 706-552-2393.

Magnolia Springs

Crystal waters bubbling out of the earth at the rate of nine million gallons a day have made this site a landmark since long before Columbus. Remnants of the Civil War prison camp that once housed ten thousand Yankees can still be found around the 948 acres that surrounded the sweetwater springs. Take the nature trails or rent a canoe to slide silently among the reedy shorelines, looking for limpkin and heron. Sandhill crane are sometimes seen; the patient observer may spot a ruby-throated hummingbird or a king rail. Tour the national fish hatchery nearby (see Bo Ginn above) to see how fingerlings are nurtured for release into the wild.

Where: Five miles north of Millen on US 25.
Facilities: Tent and trailer camping, playgrounds, rental cottages, swimming pool, picnic shelters, dock, nature trails, boat and canoe rental.
For more information: Magnolia Springs State Park, Route 5, Box 488, Millen, GA 30442; 706-982-1660.

Mistletoe State Park

A comfortable cottage on Clark Hill Lake makes the perfect nature-watching perch for the family. Or take to the campground with your tent or trailer. Focus here is on the 76,000-acre Clark Hill Lake, known for its bass fishing. The name of the park springs from Mistletoe Junction, a local area where young people came to harvest mistletoe from high in the trees and sell it in town to make pocket money before Christmas. Try to spot distinctive balls of this romantic parasite high in the trees. It's identified by its round shape and deep green color, usually contrasting dramatically in both shape and color with the host tree.

Hike six miles of trails through almost 2,000 acres of gentle hills and meadows where bird watching and wildflower photography are superb. Sunsets on the lake, usually turned a ruby red by light industrial haze, are spectacular.

Where: Twelve miles north of exit 60 off I-20, on State 150.
Facilities: Picnic tables, boat launch, developed and primitive camping, swimming beach, rental cottages, hiking trails.
For more information: Mistletoe State Park, Route 1, Box 335, Appling, GA 30802; 706-541-0321.

Ogeechee Wildlife Management Area

Like most of the state's wildlife management areas, this one is managed with controlled hunts in mind, but it's open for scouting one day before the season begins. So, for nonhunters, this is an ideal time to observe wildlife at its seasonal best.

Where: Take State 16 southwest from Warrenton to Jewel and follow the signs.
Facilities: None.
For more information: Department of Natural Resources, 205 Butler Street S.E., Suite 1252, East Towers, Atlanta, GA 30334; 404-918-6400.

George L. Smith State Park

More than a thousand acres surround a historic mill, covered bridge, and millpond, where cypress trees form a perch for blue herons and white ibis. To capture the flavor of the wetlands, take the seven-mile canoe trail or seek out the farthest shores of the 412-acre lake.

Where: Four miles southeast of Twin City off State 23.

Facilities: Tent and trailer camping, boat and canoe rental, fishing, picnic shelters.
For more information: George L. Smith State Park, Box 57, Twin City, GA 30471; 706-763-2759.

Alexander H. Stephens State Historic Park

Located in the city limits of historic Crawfordsville, home of a Civil War museum and the antebellum mansion of the Vice President of the Confederacy, this leafy park offers tent and RV camping, fishing, boat rental, and picnicking.

Where: On State 22, take exit 55 off I-20.
For more information: Alexander H. Stephens State Historic Park, Box 235, Crawfordsville, GA 30631; 706-456-2602.

Also see "Georgia Power Recreation Lands" in the Introduction. Georgia Power's Lake Sinclair borders Hancock and Putnam Counties.

3

Magnolia Midlands

These are the soils that sweeten Vidalia onions. These are the fields that bear six million pounds of plump, sweet blueberries a year and lead the nation in pine gum production. These are the lakes that spawn twenty-two-pound bass. So rich is the fishery here that Indians built a primitive fish trap in the Oconee River almost three thousand years ago. It's still here.

Ten rivers, including the Altamaha, course through the gently rolling lands of the Magnolia Midlands tourism region, making it the largest watershed east of the Mississippi. One of the most significant ecosystems in Georgia, the Altamaha is tidal for as much as forty miles from the sea; its floods stretch its width for up to twelve miles. The rich soils of its floodplains and delta filled planters' granaries with rice.

The Midlands' fertile plains fall away from stately plantations and timeless villages. Training tracks for harness horses form Warhol posters in which red clay ovals are set in green meadows bordered by white fences. The only interstate,

I-16, skims briefly across the top of the region. The rest of the highways form a slow, scenic route for Atlantans who are heading for the coast.

In fields around the town of Metter (between Dublin and Savannah), see a rare shrub known as the Georgia Plume, which is found only here and in a few remote areas of South Carolina. It's especially showy the last half of June when its snowy, four-petal flowers burst into bloom.

Tens of thousands of midlands acres are reserved for timber or wildlife management, many of them open seasonally for the harvest of game. Hunting is a huge industry throughout the state and especially here. McRae-Telfair County has 35,000 acres of pine and hardwoods in wildlife management; Wayne County has set aside 100,000 acres for wildlife management and forty hunting clubs. Quail Ridge Hunting Preserve yields quail, duck, and dove. In Addison, wild boar are hunted in season.

Regardless of your feelings about hunting, it's an important sport in this area, permitted in almost all wilderness areas in some form and in some seasons. For those who hunt with modern firearms, black powder, bow and arrow, or simply with binoculars or camera, it means some of the best stalking in the east.

Big Hammock

A National Natural Landmark, this rare ecosystem is the home of dwarf oaks that are typical of the sandhills. Moist lowlands border the river and its tributaries while higher grounds support hardwood forests. Look for rare indigo snakes, endangered gopher tortoises, and blue herons, white ibis, kites, and ducks.

Where: Nine miles west of Glennville via State 144.

Gopher tortoise

Facilities: None.
For more information: Glennville Welcome Center, 134 South Main Street, Glennville, GA 30427; 912-654-2000.

Bullard Creek

Sprawled along the south bank of the lazy Altamaha River, this 16,000-acre wildlife management area abounds in riverside wildflowers, sweet lowland shrubs, and worlds of wildlife from small mammals to trophy game. Hunting is permitted in season.

Where: Take US 221 north from Hazlehurst six and a half miles, then turn right onto a dirt road marked by a sign. The check-in station is four and a half miles farther.
Facilities: Campsites, archery range.

General Coffee State Park

Seventeen Mile River flows through this steamy, 1,490-acre park, forming a cypress swamp that widens into four lakes. For the nature lover, sightings are rich and varied. With luck, you'll spot an indigo snake or a gopher tortoise, both endangered species. Hike the trails and keep track of the number of songbirds, waterfowl, snakes, turtles, and small mammals to be seen here.

Where: Six miles east of Douglas on State 32.
Facilities: Tent and trailer sites, hiking, swimmingpool and bathhouse, picnic shelters, fishing.
For more information: General Coffee State Park, Route 2, Box 83, Nicholls, GA 31554; 912-384-7082.

Gordonia-Altamaha State Park

After twenty million years at the bottom of an ancient sea, these coastal lands emerged to form a jungle home for elephants, bison, wolves, and armadillos. Today, this tiny (280-acre) gem of a park remains far from the interstates on humid plains where wildflowers, waterfowl, and lush woodlands thrive.

Where: In Reidsville off US 280.
Facilities: Tent and trailer camping, swimming pool, twelve-acre lake, picnic shelters, miniature golf, nine-hole golf course, beaver dam, observation deck.
For more information: Gordonia-Alatamaha State Park, Box 1047, Reidsville, GA 30453; 912-557-6444.

Guido Gardens

Open for walks and meditation daily, the grounds are graced with a gazebo, a chapel, and something in bloom almost every day of the year. Ask locally about Elliottia, a rare shrub found in this area.

Where: On State 121 (North Lewis Street) in Metter.
Facilities: None.
For more information: Metter Welcome Center, I-16 at exit 23, Metter, GA 30439; 912-685-6151.

Herty Nature Trail

The name honors a pioneer in the husbandry of pine forests and the turpentine and other naval stores that they produce. In this area, they're a major cash crop. Along this fragrant nature trail on the campus of Georgia Southern University, see pines of all kinds and sizes and learn about their significance in nature and industry.

Where: South of Statesboro half a mile on US 301.
Facilities: None except for those of the university.
For more information: Convention and Visitors Bureau, Box 1516, Statesboro, GA 30458; 912-681-5611 (university) or 912-489-1869 (tourism information).

Horse Creek

This privately owned preserve spreads over ten thousand acres of pines and hardwoods in its uplands and bottomland hardwoods at lower elevations. Hunting is permitted in season. Listen for the tattoo played by woodpeckers and the song of mockingbirds. You may see a phoebe or a kingbird on its perch, hawking insects. Flycatchers nest in woodpecker holes; swallows feed in open areas; crows nest in oaks and conifers; the occasional purple martin may be seen on its way to South America for the winter.

Where: Take State 117 East from Jacksonville four miles to the check-in station.
Facilities: None.
For more information: Department of Natural Resources,

205 Butler Street S.E., Suite 1252, East Towers, Atlanta, GA 30334; 404-656-6374.

Jay Bird Springs

Said to be the oldest swimming hole in Georgia, this natural spring is revered for its healing mineral waters as well as for its touristy fun. The swimming is still sweet, pure, and refreshing, with the added spice of such attractions as a country store, train rides, and miniature golf.

Where: Twelve miles south of Eastman on State 341 South.
Facilities: Store, skating rink, restaurant, cabins, camping, picnic area.
For more information: Eastman Welcome Center, 407 College Street, Eastman, GA 31023; 912-374-4723.

Muskogean Wildlife Management Area

Private owners manage these 19,000 wild acres along the Ocmulgee River. Come for the hunting in season or just to ogle the game, wildflowers, and forests typical of Georgia bottomlands. Cedar waxwings may be seen almost any time of year; the cone-shaped nest of a vireo may be spotted in a thicket; and with luck you may see a blue-winged warbler gleaning a spring bud from a treetop or snatching a spider from a twig.

Where: Take State 117 West from Jacksonville two miles and follow the signs.
For more information: Department of Natural Resources, 205 Butler Street S.E., Suite 1252, East Towers, Atlanta, GA 30334; 404-656-6374.

Phillips Natural Area

This 800-acre National Landmark is a peaceful forest filled with rare ferns, wildflowers, and shrubs. Bring a nature identification book to help you spot walking fern, hairy lip fern, lady fern, and a long list of lichen, mushrooms, and all the creatures that live among them.

Where: Ten miles southeast of Glennville off State 121.
Facilities: None.
For more information: Glennville Welcome Center, 134 South Main Street, Glennville, GA 30427; 912-654-2000.

4

Colonial Coast

Nature's gifts to Georgia are many and varied, but no region has more abundant riches than the Colonial Coast of the Southeast. Thousands of acres of estuaries, barrier islands, and wetlands are the birthplace of life itself for both land and sea. As if these endowments weren't enough, the coast also has a front-row seat on the Atlantic flyway during bird migrations spring and fall.

An uncommon bird introduced here in recent years is the majestic chachalaca, a native of the southwestern states. Now being established on the barrier islands after being displaced at home by clearing for developments and farming, this crow-size bird feeds on hackberries and builds its nest out of Spanish moss and a concealing tangle of vines.

Moorhen (gallinule) nest in moist vegetation, especially the old rice fields that have been here since the seventeenth century. Look for their red beaks among willows or alders, where they sometimes nest, and watch them diving and ducking for forage in and above the water. With luck, you'll spot a purple gallinule in a wetland, especially one that has lots of pickerel weed or waterlilies.

Leggy and quick, limpkin are often seen stalking mud-flats and shallow water for snails, mussels, bugs, and worms.

Limpkin

Coots like wetlands too, especially where they find cattails. Shy sandhill cranes, threatened and endangered, want to nest in wetlands that aren't disturbed by humans—a tall order these days. Look for their flocks at dawn, taking off from their lowland roosts to find feeding grounds in fields, marshes, and pastures.

Even when the tranquility is broken by nature's fury, this dynamic coast has a beauty all its own. Lashing waves wash the beaches clean twice a day. Fierce ocean currents scrub away the edge of one island and deposit the sands on another. The occasional hurricane can open new passes, close old ones, rechannel rivers, and rearrange old-growth forests. Yet among the mosses and sand, the explorer can find building foundations that date back to the time of the country's original thirteen colonies.

As if all this weren't enough, this region also encloses Okefenokee, so unique that describing it challenges the best thesaurus.

Let's start at the sea. As the land rises gently from the seacoast, you'll see fields of blueberries and the occasional tobacco crop. Closer to the ocean, miles of marshes turn to a shimmering bronze as the sun sets. Sand beaches rim the Atlantic. Mainland rivers, some of them tidal for miles inland, are a recreation bonanza as well as a natural wonderland.

Read up on each of the many barrier islands before venturing out. They range from crowded and commercial to patrolled, private domains where intruders are not welcome. Some are reached via Brunswick, others via Savannah, but most cannot be reached from other islands except by boat.

Constantly building here and eroding there from the surging of the sea, the islands are never static. One, Williamson Island, appeared in recent years and has built up to a mass of a couple of hundred acres that may or may not become a permanent part of the map. Thousands of others are mere sandbars where skimmers may nest for a season before moving on. On ever-changing barrier beaches, loggerhead turtles lay their eggs, then disappear.

Nowhere else in the state is the sense of history so strong—humans have inhabited the area for at least ten thousand years. Nowhere else is nature's tapestry so fully woven with varieties of sea life, waterfowl, upland birds and game, small mammals, amphibians, reptiles, plant life ranging from ancient hardwoods to steely cordgrass, and colorful blooms that keep unfurling winter and summer.

Brunswick

In town, find the historic Lover's Oak, which is thirteen feet in circumference at its base. The mammoth live oak is at the corner of Albany and Prince Streets. Separating Brunswick from the "golden" isles to the east are marshes much like those that line the entire Georgia coast between the mainland and the barrier islands. The difference is that these, called the Marshes of Glynn, were made famous by poet Sidney Lanier. At an overlook park along US 17, you'll find picnic tables.

Where: write the Visitors Bureau, 4 Glynn Avenue, Brunswick, GA 31520; 912-264-5337. Request a list of wildlife management areas, most of them reedy marshlands where bird-watchers can check off dozens of species in a day. Don't overlook smaller treasures too: butterflies, colorful insects, and shallows bright with darting bait fish. The management areas, which allow hunting in season, include:

Atkinson Tract. Go north on US 341 to Everett City, right on Altamaha Park Road for two and eight-tenths miles, then right at the sign.

Harrington Tract. Take US 341 north to State 32, then go left for thirteen and a half miles to Post Road and left for two and three-tenths miles to the sign.

Hazzard's Neck is a 12,000-acre tract near Crooked Neck State Park, St. Marys. From Brunswick, take US 17 south thirteen miles to Dover Bluff Road, go five and five-tenths miles to Waverly Road, then go left one and six-tenths miles to the sign.

Sansville Tract. Go north on US 341 to Mt. Pleasant and turn right across the railroad track into the wildlife management area.

Tyler Tract. Go north on US 341 to Mt. Pleasant, turn left onto Post Road, and go two and three-tenths miles to the dirt road on your right.

Bonaventure Cemetery

One of the loveliest gardens in the state, where azaleas and camellias bloom and centuries-old live oaks trail yards of Spanish moss over old gravestones, this burial ground is the final resting place of many of Savannah's most famous citizens and soldiers including Noble Jones (see Wormsloe at the end of this chapter).

Wisteria, which looks and smells like lilac, grows here on woody vines while saucer-size magnolias add their distinctive perfume to an enchanted scene first described by naturalist John Muir in 1867.

Where: Along the Wilmington River on Bonaventure Road via US 80 to Mechanics Avenue. Open daylight hours, free.
For more information: Convention and Visitors Bureau, 222 West Oglethorpe Street, Savannah 31402; 800-444-2427 or 912-9440426.

Crooked River State Park

Just barely above the Florida border, this coastal park basks in warm winters on the banks of Crooked River. Explore by canoe the shoreline of a 412-acre lake and on seven miles of canoe trails. Or walk through ruins of a tabby sugar mill that was built early in the 1800s.

Along the banks look for stands of the fever tree (pinckneya), which was also called the headache tree by early settlers. Used in bush medicine, it's said to contain the same chemical found in aspirin. In springtime, look for trillium. Yellow flytrap, a protected wildflower, also grows here. It's one of six rare, colorful pitcher plants found in this area. Meat-eating flytraps, they survive by filling their "pitchers" with water for trapping and digesting insects.

Where: Ten miles north of St. Marys on Georgia Spur 40, east of Kingsland twelve miles off US 17 or eight miles off I-95.
Facilities: Tent and trailer campsites, picnic shelter, boat and canoe rentals.
For more information: Crooked River State Park, 3092 Spur 40, St. Marys, GA 31558; 912-882-5256.

Cumberland Island National Seashore

A sixteen mile-long finger of land that shelters mainland Georgia from the lapping Atlantic, this wildly beautiful barrier island was settled centuries ago but has reverted almost completely to nature's whims. Wild horses and feral donkeys graze the meadows. Raccoons, deer, wild boar, and possum watch warily as day-trippers walk through forests of huge live oaks and tangled tupelo. Here and there in the wilderness you'll spot an old foundation, chimney, or an Indian shell mound.

Indian settlements flourished here for at least three thousand years before the arrival of the Spanish, who established a Christian mission in the mid-1500s. It probably endured for eighty years or more. In 1739, Cumberland was fortified by the English against the Spanish, who were routed in the nearby Battle of Bloody Marsh, then was abandoned for decades.

Modern tenants included Revolutionary War General Nathanael Greene, whose estate, Dungeness, sheltered another war hero, Harry "Light-Horse" Lee after he became ill while sailing off the Georgia coast in 1818. He died here and was buried at Dungeness Cemetery until 1913, when his remains were removed to Virginia to lie next to the body of his son, Robert E. Lee.

The mansion built here by Lacy Carnegie as a wedding present for her son at the end of the nineteenth century has been restored by the National Park Service. Take a tour for a glimpse of the way this family was living on Cumberland during the heydays of the millionaires' hunting club on nearby Jekyll Island.

Only a tiny parcel of the island remains today in private ownership. Greyfield Inn is a nine-room bed and breakfast that can accommodate outsiders occasionally for meals. Reservations must be made a week in advance. For all other information and services, contact the National Park Service.

If you take the morning ferry and keep on the move all day until the afternoon pick-up, it's possible to hike across the island to the beach, enjoy a swim and a picnic, then hike up the beach to connect with the other cross-island trail back to the river. In summer, when bugs, humidity, and heat are at their zenith, don't plan too ambitious a day. If you miss the return ferry, you're stranded.

The Dungeness Trail, which begins at the docks on the lee side of the island, leads through various habitats, starting with a typical maritime forest that lines the "avenue" that leads from the dock. Look beyond the Spanish moss for small, pineapple-like clusters of air plants. Some types produce tiny, colorful blooms. Also found in the live oaks and pines is the Resurrection plant, which is sometimes found for sale in gift shops. Seemingly brown and dead when it's dry, it swells to a plump green after a good rain.

Walk through the woods, which also have stands of American holly, magnolia, cedar, and cabbage palm, to look for raccoons, white-tailed deer, armadillos, and lots of gray squirrels. Occasionally, on the forest floor, elusive wild turkeys will be spotted by the sharp-eyed observer. A turkey nests in a depression at the base of a tree or shrub, emerging to grab a meal of grasshoppers, walkingsticks, seeds, and grains.

The path continues along the salt marsh, where cordgrass decomposes to a rich detritus that feeds thick beds of clams, fiddler crabs, oysters, shrimps, and periwinkles. Marsh wrens, rails, and seaside sparrows make nests in the grasses while osprey, pelicans, and other fisher birds soar overhead and leggy shorebirds work the shallows.

The trail is one of two that ends at the broad, sandy beach with its fringe of sea oats. (Don't cross the dunes except at designated spots.) Along the way, you'll pass an old family cemetery and outbuildings that were once worked by two hundred servants who operated a lavish, self-sufficient estate for the Carnegies.

There's also a trail along the river between the two docks and the Nightingale Trail through interdune meadows that brim with life. Keep an eye out for marsh rabbits and for white-tailed deer hiding in wax-myrtle thickets.

Where: Tour boats leave from the waterfront, St. Marys. For more on St. Marys, write to the Park Superintendent, Box 806, St. Marys, GA 31558; 912-882-4335. Reservations for the boat tour and overnight camping are essential; federal law limits the number of visitors allowed here each day. Ferry hours vary in season; the park is closed during short hunting seasons held for a few days at a time from November to January.

Facilities: Primitive camping, mansion tours. Both campers

and day visitors must bring everything they'll need while on the island, including fresh water. Fires are permitted only in designated areas, so it's best to bring a camp stove. Permits are required for camping the backcountry.
For more information: Write the Tourism Council Inc., 414 Osborne Street, St. Marys, GA 31558. For reservations to spend the night at the Greyfield Inn or for dining there when space permits, call 904-261-6408.

Fort King George

This strategic spot on the Altamaha River has been occupied and fortified since long before European settlement. Evidence of human habitation here goes back ten thousand years or more. The earliest British defenders realized its strategic importance. Today, uniformed Redcoats give guided tours of the reconstructed blockhouse and palisades. Despite centuries of intrusion, however, much of the area looks much as it did centuries ago.

Walk the mile-long nature trail through typical Low Country terrain, humid but breezy. Ruins of sawmills tell the story of timbering here: oak and pine were hauled away by the thousands of board feet. Today, look for young oaks and pines plus entire families of bayberry, cottonwood, sweetbay, hawthorn, sweetgum, black locust, and sumac.

Where: In Darien, three miles east of exit 10 off I-95.
Facilities: Rest rooms, museum, nature path, historical reconstructions.
For more information: Fort King George State Historic Site, Box 711, Darien, GA 31305; 912-437-4770. Admission. Closed Mondays, some holidays.

Fort McAllister and Richmond Hill

The earthworks here along the Ogeechee River were crucial to the defense of Savannah during the Civil War, and they fell to General Sherman in 1864. Today, they are just pleasant overlooks where sojourners can hike the nature trails, camp, picnic, or fish this side-by-side historic site and state park.

Typical of the rich coastal habitat, the parks offer a variety of forest and bogs. Take a field guide to help you identify cedar and cypress, hickory and oak, bayberry and osage orange. Wildflower seekers can catalog such finds as wild pansy, violets, jewelweed, wild morning glory, sparkling Indian pipes, and more than half a dozen species of wild orchids.

Where: Ten miles east of I-95 on State 144.
Facilities: Tent and trailer camping, dock, boat ramp, picnic shelters. Wheelchair access is good throughout except at the fort entrance, where some help may be needed.
For more information: Fort McAllister State Historic Park, Route 2 Box 394-A, Richmond Hill, GA 31324; 912-727-2339.
Also: A 172-acre tract along the Ogeechee River about ten miles upstream from the river mouth is owned by the Savannah Science Museum, 4405 Paulsen Street, Savannah, GA 31402; 912-355-6705. Logged out about thirty years ago, it is gradually returning to nature as hardwoods reforest the swampy bottomland and pines and palmetto return to the sandhill ridge. Wildflowers are spectacular, especially in springtime when the sparkleberry blooms. Call the museum for instructions on accessing the tract because private owners nearby are very sensitive about intruders.

Forsyth Park

One of the prettiest of Savannah's formal, London-like parks, this one has a fragrance garden for the blind and a network of walking/jogging paths.

Where: Gaston and Park Avenues.
Facilities: None.
For more information: Convention and Visitors Bureau, 222 West Oglethorpe Street, Savannah, GA 31402; 800-444-2427 or 912-944-0426. Request walking maps of the city, which is dotted with twenty-one half-acre parks, each centered with a fountain or statue and landscaped with fine lawns, flowering shrubs and trees, annuals, and shade trees.

Fort Morris

Rivers of reeds glow golden in the sun along this ancient coast, which reverted to its natural state after the British destroyed their village and fort when they left in 1782. All that remains today are old earthworks that served in both the Revolutionary War and the War of 1812. The colonial port city of Sunbury, once a bustling harbor, lives on only in exhibits in the small museum (see later in this chapter).

Where: Seven miles east of I-95 exit 13 via State 38.
Facilities: Picnic area, restrooms, museum.
For more information: Fort Morris State Historic Site, Route 1, Box 236, Midway, GA 31320; 912-884-5999. Closed Mondays; hours vary. Call ahead.

Fort Pulaski

Primarily a historic monument under the National Park Service, the fort's location at the entrance to the Savannah River makes it a nature watcher's destination, too. High hammocks overlook the salt marshes and rich estuarine wetlands, providing excellent bird-watching for species ranging from songbirds to long-legged heron and strutting beach scavengers.

One of the trails is a short nature loop among historic sites. Another borders the marshes, and a third follows an antebellum dike that was surveyed by a young Robert E. Lee.

Where: Fifteen miles east of Savannah off US 80.
Facilities: Historic buildings, museum, nature trails, picnicking, boat ramp, fishing, ranger-led tours.
For more information: Superintendent, Fort Pulaski, Box 30757, Savannah, GA 31410; 912-786-5787.

Harris Neck National Wildlife Refuge

A plantation once spread over much of this 2,765-acre reserve along the South Newport River. The Lorillards of tobacco fame used it as a country refuge before the turn of the century; the U.S. Air Force put in runways during World War II and used it as a training field. The remains of the landing field, which make a good photo platform, can still be seen on high ground in the salt marsh and forests.

Thanks to its previous tenants, the area has fifteen miles of paved roads, including an eight-mile, self-guided route through woods and fields. Take your time, watching for native nesting species that include a dozen types of ducks and a spectrum of wading birds plus visiting and accidental birds such as spotted red hawks, snow buntings, and roseate spoonbills. The Refuge is more marsh than land, making it a mecca for waterfowl.

Where: Take exit 12 off I-95 (South Newport River) and go south a mile on US 17 to State 131, then left (east) for seven miles to the refuge entrance.
Note: Write or phone for maps and instructions before you go. Controlled hunts are scheduled, and some areas may also be closed at times for managed burns or floods. Check ahead.
Facilities: Self-guided driving, bicycling, or walking tour.
For more information: Mailing address: Harris Neck National Wildlife Refuge, National Park Service S.E. Region, Russell Office Building, Room 1004, 75 Spring Street, Atlanta, GA 30303; 404-652-4415.

Roseate spoonbill

Hofwyl-Broadfield Plantation

Once a rice plantation along the Altamaha River, these acres are now of interest primarily for the old plantation home and buildings. However, nature lovers will want to wander the grounds to marvel at the size of the live oaks, the beauty of the magnolias and camellias, the silvery richness of the Spanish moss, and the vastness of marshes that were once rice paddies tended by more than three hundred slaves.

Where: Between Brunswick and Darien on US 17, one mile east of I-95 exit 9.
Facilities: Museum, slide show, restrooms. Closed Mondays. Sunday hours 2 to 5 P.M. Admission.
For more information: Hofwyl-Broadfield Plantation, Route 10, Box 83, Brunswick, GA 31520; 912-264-9263.

Jekyll Island

A perfect compromise between the resorty islands and those that have no facilities at all is this state-owned island with limited development. Rent bicycles and explore winding roads through canopies of live oaks. Don't miss the Historic District, a tourist area that deserves listing in this book because of its impressive live oaks, an Indian mound, and the old marina where you can gaze out over the marshes while sipping a sundowner or feasting on local seafood. The beaches are a perfect seascape of sugary sand and delicate sea oats.
Where: Take the Jekyll Island Causeway from Brunswick.
Mailing Address: Jekyll Island Authority, 375 Riverview Drive, Brunswick, GA 31527.
For more information: Call the Convention and Visitors Bureau, 800-841-6586 or 912-635-4080.

Little Satilla

Along Little Satilla Creek, a 15,000-acre wildlife management area is hunted in season. From Patterson, take State 32 east four miles and follow the yellow signs.

Facilities: None.
For more information: Department of Natural Resources, 205 Butler St. S.E., Atlanta, GA 30334; 404-656-3522.

Oatland Island Education Center

A magnificent 175-acre tract, the center has nature trails through ten habitats where you can observe plants and animals native to this part of the Low Country. There's also a petting zoo of farm animals. Walkways allow easy viewing of the marshes.

Where: 711 Sandtown Road, Savannah.
Facilities: Restrooms, historic log cabins.
For more information: Convention and Visitors Bureau, Box 1628, Savannah, GA 31402; 800-444-2427 or 912-944-0456. Admission is a can of Alpo dog food.

Okefenokee National Wildlife Refuge

Early Indians called it the Land of Trembling Earth because much of the land was afloat, unattached to the deep ooze below. It took centuries for seedlings to turn into trees that sent out deep taproots that eventually anchored these islands to the earth.

Today, this 438,000-acre National Wildlife Refuge is not only the largest but the most ecologically intact of its type in the United States. The nature watching here defies superlatives. See bay trees covered in white blooms, brilliant waterlilies and yellow spatterdock afloat on black waters, and the dewy blue of pickerelweed and wild iris along marshy shorelines.

In moist bogs, look for common and rare species of

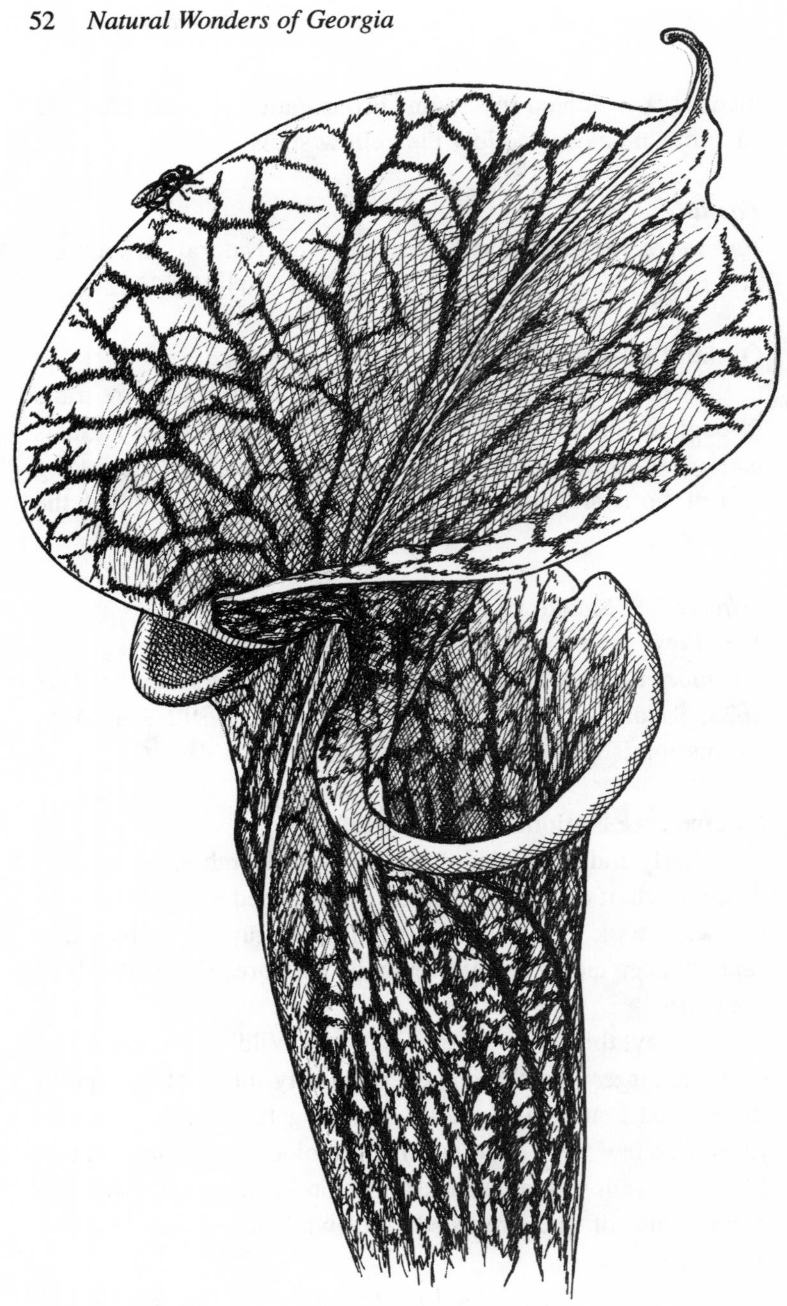

Pitcher plant

pitcher plants, which trap and devour insects. On drier ground, look for the prickly pear cactus with its waxy yellow bloom in spring and sweet red "pears" in late summer.

Spend quiet hours on footpaths and canoe trails to look for round-tailed muskrats, alligators, raccoons, turtles, and worlds of waterfowl. A few bald cypresses grow among the more common pond cypresses, forming aeries for raptors and bats. Mockingbirds and Carolina wrens make their homes in upland trees. Thousands of acres of prairies form rookeries for sandhill cranes, herons, egrets, and ducks of all colors.

Threading through the swamp are countless miles of trails, boardwalks, and canoe trails, including a hundred-mile, self-guided canoe trail with lean-tos at overnight camping spots. Reservations can be made for trips of two to five days. A caveat: Heat, humidity, and insects are among the natural wonders of Georgia. In Okefenokee, the bugs are exceptionally wondrous. No matter what time of year you visit, take plenty of sportsman's-strength repellents for biting flies, ticks, and mosquitoes.

For more information: Okefenokee National Wildlife Refuge, Route 2, Box 338, Folkston, GA 31537; 912-496-3331. Access to the Refuge is via areas that include the following:

Okefenokee Heritage Center provides excellent orientation for wilderness-bound explorers. Focus is on the Okefenokee's relationship with humankind: Indians, pioneer homes and artifacts, social-science exhibits, an 1812 train depot, and an art gallery. On the grounds are nature trails. Heritage center is off US 82, two miles west of Waycross; 912-285-4260.

For more information: Refuge Manager, Okefenokee National Wildlife Refuge, Route 2, Box 338, Folkston, GA 31537; 912-496-3331.

S.C. Foster State Park, on Jones Island at one of the primary entrances to Okefenokee, gives visitors easy access to the edges of this untamed swamp. Walk the half-mile nature trail, take a guided boat trip across dark waters that are home to sixty amphibians and fifty-four reptiles, and walk the boardwalk across teeming wetlands. The park's moist, warm environment hosts forty-one species of animals and two hundred and twenty-three species of birds. Because it's on the Suwannee River, the park is named for Stephen Foster, who, ironically, never saw the river he made famous.

Where: Eighteen miles northwest of Fargo via State 177.
Facilities: Tent and trailer campsites, interpretive center, picnic shelters, rental cottages, boat rental, guided boat tours, educational programs.
For more information: S.C. Foster State Park, Route 1, Box 131, Fargo, GA 31631; 912-637-5274.

Okefenokee Swamp Park is a nonprofit development under long-term lease, supported by private funds. In providing convenient entry, guides, and access, the facility allows ordinary tourists to approach a wilderness that less-hardy visitors don't care to tackle. Take the boat tour, which varies in length according to water levels, and visit the interpretive center for exhibits, films, and lectures. Climb the observation tower for a bird's-eye view of the swamp. This park and Laura S. Walker State Park are both within the Waycross State Forest.
Where: Eight miles south of Waycross on US 1 and 23.
Facilities: Picnic area, canoe rental, displays. Overnight in Waycross or at Laura S. Walker State Park. Hours vary seasonally. Admission.
For more information: Okefenokee Swamp Park, 5700 Okefenokee Swamp Road, Waycross, GA 31501; 912-283-0583.

Laura S. Walker State Park is a separate, 306-acre preserve but geographically, it can be considered a part of the Okefenokee Swamp, with much the same flora and fauna. It also provides access to Dixon Memorial Forest.

Where: Nine miles southeast of Waycross on State 177.
Facilities: Tent and trailer camping, lake, pool, picnic shelters, nature trail, fishing dock, canoe rental.
For more information: Laura L. Walker State Park, 5653 Laura Walker Road, Waycross, GA 31501; 912-287-4900.

Suwanee Canal Recreation Area is the entry to four prairie habitats within the Okefenokee swamp that are dotted with small lakes and gator ponds. Rent a boat or bicycle or take a guided tour. The entrance is eleven miles southwest of Folkston off State 23/121. Call 912-496-7836.
For more information: Park Manager, Okefenokee National Wildlife Refuge, Route 2, Box 338, Folkston, GA 31537; 912-496-3331.

Ossabaw Island

It takes advance planning to visit this remote, wind-sculpted State Heritage Reserve south of Savannah. It is managed by the Department of Natural Resources for its cultural, natural, and scientific resources, which range from a healthy deer herd to archaeological finds among old tabby ruins. If you have a boat, you can land here without a permit as long as you stay below the high-tide line.

Bird life is especially rich and abundant, with the usual cast of sea and shore birds plus a shy bluebird population. Brackish ponds support families of beaver, mink, and otter. Feral donkeys and hogs, left behind by people who once farmed the island, continue to survive and breed in the wild. Hunting is permitted for a short season in winter; fishing and crabbing along the shores and in the sounds are fruitful.

For more information: Department of Natural Resources, 205 Butler Street S.E., Atlanta, GA 30334; 404-656-3522; Sapelo Island Game Management Office, 1 Conservation Way, Brunswick, GA 31523; 912-262-3173. Inquire about access, permits, seasons, regulations, and any licenses you may need.

St. Catherines Island

One of Georgia's most dramatically high and scenic barrier islands, St. Catherines is also one of the most inaccessible unless you have your own boat or can connect with a field trip through a school or conservation group. The island is rich in human history that began with the Guale Indians, who made it their tribal capital, and continued with the Spanish, whose mission here in the sixteenth century was the northernmost post they established in the New World. Button Gwinnett, one of the signers of the Declaration of Independence, owned and farmed the island during the mid 1700s. A free black colony was established here before the Civil War.

Buildings and foundations, some of them excavated in the 1980s by a team of professional archaeologists, can be found but are off-limits to visitors except by special arrangement. If you go in your own boat, keep in mind that public access extends only to the high-tide line.

Through its long association with academia, St. Catherines has also been used as a breeding ground for rare animals such as hartebeests and lemurs and as a sea-turtle monitoring station. So, while it takes advance planning to arrange a field trip here, nature observers are rewarded with the usual barrier-island beaches, birds, and wildlife, plus a peek at a long list of ongoing studies and experiments.

Where: Between Ossabaw and Sapelo Islands, southeast of Savannah.
For more information: St. Catherines Foundation, Route 1, Box 207, Midway, GA 31320; 912-884-5002.

St. Simons and Little St. Simons Islands

Here, at the Battle of Bloody Marsh, the British decisively

defeated the Spanish in 1742 and kept Georgia safe for English settlers. Like Jekyll, St. Simons has been prudently developed so that nature lovers can find plenty of solitude as well as upscale lodgings.

Drive or bicycle to the marinas around the island for scenes of shrimpers and small boats set among seas of reeds and wandering waterways. At Gascoigne Bluff, timbers were cut to build *Old Ironsides*. Throughout these islands, note the way the sea winds have sculpted the limbs of live oaks into natural ribs and knees, and you can see why these forests had strategic value to early shipbuilders.

The island is studded with parks, edged with a superb beach, and blessed with some of the state's oldest and best historic sites, including Fort Frederica, built by Georgia founder James Oglethorpe in 1736. Even if you're not a historian, visit the tree-shaded grounds to study the mosses and native weeds.

Climb the one hundred and twenty-nine steps to the top of the lighthouse (c. 1872) and visit the little museum in the lighthouse-keeper's cottage. Retreat Plantation, renowned for the fine quality of its Sea Island cotton, is now a golf course, but the remains of a slave hospital can still be seen.

Where: The toll road to St. Simons is north of Brunswick off US 17. Entering the south end of the island, stop at the visitor center or call ahead, 912-638-9014 or 800-525-8687.
For more information: Visitor Center, Neptune Park, St. Simons Island, GA 31522.

Little St. Simons Island, with its six miles of unspoiled beach, is still privately owned, but now has a small inn from which guests can observe bird life, look for seashells, ride horseback through the surf, or canoe the marshes. It's reached only by boat. Occasionally, special weekend events present wine tastings, herb gatherings, or seminars. Call 912-638-7472.

For more information: Little St. Simons Island, Box 1078, St. Simons, GA 31522.

Sapelo Island National Estuarine Sanctuary

The first Europeans arrived on this low-lying island in the early sixteenth century. It was purchased from Indian princess Mary Musgrove by the British Crown in 1760 and was planted in Sea Island cotton and sugar cane by English and French settlers. To tour the unique estuarine environment, cross to the island aboard the *Sapelo Queen* and see marsh and beach ecosystems, the community of Hog Hammock, centuries-old tabby ruins, and all the plants and birdlife common to these islands, as well as the University of Georgia Marine Research Institute.

Where: Write the Chamber of Commerce, Box 1497, Darien, GA 31305; 912-437-6684 or 437-4192. Tour schedules vary with the season, with half-day tours available June through Labor Day and full-day tours offered once a month March through October. Reservations required.

Blackbeard Island National Wildlife Refuge

Lying off Sapelo Island, Blackbeard Island is accessible only by boat. Said to have been frequented by the pirate himself, the island has been in government hands since 1800. First, it was harvested for its live-oak timbers during an era when the oak's iron hardness made for stout warships. The government handed the island down for use as a quarantine station; then it was made a wildlife refuge by President Woodrow Wilson and a natural refuge by President Franklin D. Roosevelt.

Here, nature provides a perfect salt marsh and shore habitat for egrets, herons, sandpipers, gulls, and ospreys. Mazes of golden marsh offer endless exploring at a slow pace.

Stop often to listen to the buzz of bird, insect, and sea life at work in one of nature's most prolific nurseries.

Where: Darien Welcome Center, Box 1497, Darien, GA 31305, or stop at the welcome center at the foot of the Darien River Bridge on US 17; 912-437-4192. Guided tours are available.
Facilities: None.
For more information: U.S. Fish and Wildlife Service, Box 8487, Savannah, GA 31412; 912-944-4415. From the same address, request information on the Harris Neck National Wildlife Refuge, Savannah Natural Wildlife Refuge, Wassaw Island National Wildlife Refuge, and Wolf Island National Wildlife Refuge.

Savannah National Wildlife Refuge

Most of this 25,600-acre refuge lies north of the state line in South Carolina, and most of it can be reached only by boat. It's a superb frontier for canoeists to explore along the Savannah River past paddies that once grew rice and now form a perfect habitat for waterfowl and alligators. For land explorers, the best viewing is from the four-mile Laurel Hill Wildlife Drive, a loop tour off US 17 at the river. There's also a two-mile walking path two miles north on US 321, and the dikes are open during daylight hours (except where posted) to hikers and bikers.

The refuge shows two dramatic faces to visitors: Huge industrial installations form a strange symmetry against the skyline while, in other areas, only nature's profile is seen—forests of cypress and live oak. Mankind has been exploiting this resource since the earliest settlers built dams and canals to form rice fields; today, they're all part of a complex that creates a habitat for fish, birds, deer, wild boar, and wildlife of all kinds.

Alligator

In season, the refuge is open for managed hunts. Some areas are closed to all visitors from November through early March, to protect waterfowl that winter here.

Where: Take the first exit off I-95 north of the Savannah River in South Carolina. Guided tours of the Refuge are available out of Savannah. Contact the Convention and Visitors Bureau, 222 West Oglethorpe Street, Savannah, GA 31402; 800-444-2427 or 912-944-0426.
Facilities: Welcome center, educational displays, hiking and bicycling paths, drinking water, restrooms.
For more information: Savannah National Wildlife Refuge,

U.S. Fish and Wildlife Service, 75 Spring Street, Atlanta, GA 30303; 404-331-3588.

Savannah Science Museum

This is the place to acquaint yourself with all the amphibians, reptiles, birds, minerals, plants, seashells, and rocks you'll encounter in the Low Country. Live, stuffed, and static displays delight all ages; there's also a planetarium.

Where: Savannah Science Museum, 4405 Paulsen Street, Savannah, GA 31400; 912-355-6705.
Facilities: Restrooms, souvenir shop. Hours vary. Admission.

Sea Island

Geographically, Sea Island is as rich in natural wonders as the other Golden Isles, but don't venture to this very private, ultra-exclusive island unless you're a guest at The Cloister or one of the private estates here. Security is tight to protect the sitting and past U.S. presidents and other VIPs who vacation here. Intruders are not welcome.

Where: Sea Island is reached from St. Simons Island. For reservations at The Cloister, Georgia's only five-star resort and one of the finest seaside retreats in the nation, call 912-638-3611 or 800-SEA-ISLA.
For more information: Brunswick and the Golden Isles, 4 Glynn Avenue, Brunswick, GA 31520; 912-265-0630 or 800-933-COAST.

Skidaway Island State Park

Once hooked on Georgia's Golden Isles, you'll want to explore them all. This one is a birder's paradise only six miles from Savannah, a 506-acre reserve of marshes, tidal flats, and estuarine waters that leap and swirl with sea life.

Walk the nature trails to look for the blooms of Cherokee rose, a native shrub that grows among the palmetto scrub, as well as yaupon holly and cabbage palms. One trail is a mile-long loop; another totals five miles through a grand variety of hardwood high grounds, marshes, and Civil War-era earthworks.

Where: On Diamond Causeway, six miles southeast of Savannah. Take I-16 to I-516, then exit 34 onto DeRenne Avenue, go right on Waters Avenue and straight ahead to the Causeway.
Facilities: Tenting, RV camping, picnic shelters, playground, swimming pool, education programs, nature trails, horseshoes, volleyball.
For more information: Skidaway Island State Park, Savannah 31406; 912-598-2300 or 912-598-2301. Park hours 7 A.M. to 10 P.M., office 8 A.M. to 5 P.M.

Skidaway Marine Science Complex

On historic Modena Plantation on the Skidaway River, the complex has a twelve-thousand-gallon aquarium and exhibits that include archaeological finds from the area's earliest human residents. European settlement here dates to as early as 1736, three years after the founding of Georgia, when preacher John Wesley, a founder of the Methodist faith, visited the island.

See tanks of Atlantic coastal species, including pompano, nurse shark, and turtles. Also on display are an extensive shell collection and the skeleton of a sperm whale that beached itself near here in the 1950s. Study the model of Gray's Reef, one of the region's richest fisheries, to learn how it evolved during the Ice Age. It lies deep in the ocean off Georgia.

Where: Take Skidaway Island Drive to the Red Building at the end of McWhirter Drive. Open Monday to Friday 9 A.M. to 4 P.M.; 912-598-2496.
Facilities: Restrooms (not wheelchair accessible).
For more information: Convention and Visitors Bureau, Box 1628, Savannah, GA 31402; 800-444-2427 or 912-944-0456.

George L. Smith State Park

More than a thousand acres surround a historic mill, covered bridge, and millpond where cypress trees form a perch for blue herons and white ibis. To capture the flavor of the wetlands, take the seven-mile canoe trail or seek out the farthest shores of the 412-acre lake.

Where: Four miles southeast of Twin City off State 23.
Facilities: Tent and trailer camping, boat and canoe rental, fishing, picnic shelters.
For more information: George L. Smith State Park, Box 57, Twin City, GA 30471; 912-763-2759.

Southern Forest World

In a state where the harvest of pine trees is a major industry, the science of forestry is taken seriously. Here, in a warren of nature trails through native timber, ferns, and wildflowers, an exhibit tells the story of forestry in Georgia and twelve other southern states.

Where: In Waycross on North Augusta Avenue between US 1 and 82, next to the Okefenokee Heritage Center.
For more information: Southern Forest World, Route 5, Box 406B, Waycross, GA 31502; 912-285-4056.

Sunbury

The once-flourishing town of Sunbury is another of the parks along the Colonial Coast that is better known for its historic interest than its natural wonders, but it's well worth a visit for the boardwalk and overlook on the Medway River and St. Catherines Sound. Another early settlement that could not be sustained against storms and periodic scourges of yellow fever, the town was already in decline by the close of the War of 1812.

Visit the museum to learn about the flora and fauna of this part of the Low Country. Walk the nature path to see the remains of the old fortifications, now incongruously dotted with mature trees and shrubs. Along a lonely footpath, surprise a family of quail—mother followed by half a dozen chicks. Look for nut trees, probably descendants of those planted by early settlers: pecan, black walnut, hickory, chestnuts. On the boardwalk overlooking the river, you're sure to see loons, shearwaters, pelicans, herons, and a variety of swans, ducks, and geese.

Where: Sunbury State Historic Site is east of I-95 off State 38.
Facilities: Restrooms, exhibits.
For more information: Georgia Dept. of State Parks and Historic Sites, 205 Butler Street SE Suite 1352, Darien, GA 31305; 912-437-4770.

Tuckahoe Wildlife Management Area

Hunters and anglers know about this 11,000-acre tract on the Savannah River, but nature observers who are willing to rough it can also discover the wild wonders of the wetlands here. Roads once cleared by timber companies form the only access to a wilderness ruled by alligators, wild pigs, deer, quail, small game, and a full spectrum of upland game birds, waterfowl, and songbirds.

Where: Take State 24 east from Sylvania to County 243 and County 127.
Facilities: None.
For more information: Department of Natural Resources, 205 Butler Street S.E., Atlanta, GA 30334; 404-656-3522.

Tybee Island

Only seventeen miles east of Savannah, Tybee Island is a busy, price-appealing vacation spot filled with amusements and small motels. Still, you can find room to build a sand castle or feed the seagulls, especially on weekdays and in off-seasons when the bird life is often at its most active.

Actually a cluster of islands, Tybee is a popular spot for crabbing and for fishing in the surf, from the pier or from a deep-sea charter boat.

Stop at the visitors center to get information on the lighthouse, where you can huff and puff up the three hundred steps to the top for a bird's-eye view. The latest of several lights that have stood here since before the Revolutionary War, it's still a working lighthouse. Visit the Marine Science Center and Museum, too, checking ahead because hours vary according to season. Fort Screven, which dates to 1875, is open daily except Tuesday in winter, daily in summer.

Where: Take US 80 from Savannah and stop at the visitors center on US 80. It's open daily except Monday. For information, call 912-786-5444.
For more information: Convention and Visitors Bureau, 222 West Oglethorpe Avenue, Savannah, GA 31402; 912-944-0456.

Wassaw Island National Wildlife Refuge

Accessible only by boat, this 10,000-acre island and its sister, Pine Island, are disturbed more by the thundering waves of the Atlantic than by the tread of humans. Barrier islands that take the constant pounding of the tireless sea, Wassaw and Pine erode and build depending on the whim of the waves, which continue to gnaw at the ruins of a fort that was built during the Spanish-American War in 1898.

If you have your own boat, use the U.S. Fish and Wildlife Service's dock along Wassaw Creek near the southern end of the island. Sea kayakers also like to visit Wassaw, paddling down the Wilmington River to Skidaway Island, then sometimes venturing on to Wassaw. Commercial boats also run to the island from several points in the area, usually with a stop at the beach. Part of the former owner's deal in ceding this island to the state was that a bridge would never be built.

Seemingly impenetrable, the island is actually threaded by twenty miles of trails through one of the finest virgin maritime forests in the nation. The unhurried nature watcher (preferably well slathered with bug spray) will have many sightings of deer, alligators, amphibians of all kinds, rabbits, and otters. Migratory birds abound in spring and fall, and heron nest near the dunes. The beaches are spectacular, not just for swimming and surf fishing but also for nature watching, shelling, and watching the shorebirds play tag with the waves in their search for meaty shells.

For more information: Wassaw Island National Wildlife Refuge, c/o U.S. Fish and Wildlife Service, 75 Spring Street SW, Atlanta, GA 30303

Also Convention and Visitors Bureau, 222 West Oglethorpe Street, Savannah, GA 31402; 800-444-2427 or 912-944-0426.

Woodmanston Plantation

The rich bottomlands here were planted to rice only a few decades after the founding of Georgia. Woodmanston

Plantation flourished well into the nineteenth century, when intense logging began. The home of one of Georgia's most distinguished families, Louis LeConte and his sons John and Joseph, Woodmanston Plantation attracted botanists from all over the world to see the beautiful gardens that flourished here in the eighteenth and nineteenth centuries. It was here that the LeConte pear was developed. Beloved educators who ended up on the West Coast, the LeConte brothers are honored in a dozen school names including LeConte Hall on the University of California campus at Berkeley. Eventually the mansion and the splendid botanical gardens planted early in the 1800s were reclaimed by nature. Now the grounds have been restored and are the site of an annual Rice Festival in April. Highlighted by a regal alley of oaks, the nature trail is a showplace of flowering shrubs, native trees, ferns, and bird life.

Where: Woodmanston Plantation is west of Riceboro. Take exit 12 or 13 off I-95, then go west on US 17. Inquire locally when you get to Riceboro, either at the Midway Museum (on US 17 six miles north of Riceboro; 912-884-5837) or, when it's closed, at local merchants.
For more information: Convention and Visitors Bureau, 222 West Oglethorpe Street, Savannah, GA 31402; 800-444-2427 or 912-944-0426.

Wormsloe, State Historic Site

This historic site is sought out today for its tabby ruins and its living-history demonstrations of everyday colonial life. Nature's graces, however, are the things that have attracted visitors here since pre-Revolutionary times. Walk a mile-long nature trail through native azaleas, magnolias, and dogwoods to look for raccoons, squirrels, and coastal songbirds.

Noble Jones, a physician and carpenter from Surrey, England, came to Georgia aboard the ship *Anne* in 1733 with

---

ABOUT THE WOOD STORK

One of the largest and most interesting of the rare or endangered species that can be observed in this region by the patient and persistent nature lover is the bird that is variously called the wood stork, wood ibis, or flinthead. A massive three and a half feet tall, it has a wingspan of five feet or more and a bill that may be as long as nine inches.

If you're lucky enough to witness a mating ceremony, it begins when a male stakes out a nesting spot and starts challenging any other wood stork that appears. If it is a rival male, it will snap back. If it's a female, she approaches with her bill in an open gape, her wings spread. If the attraction is mutual, they greet each other with gaping bills, raising and lowering their heads in the wood-stork way of welcome.

Wood storks nest in colonies that can number in the hundreds, in cypress swamps on platforms they build high in trees. They construct their nests with sticks and line them with leaves and twigs, creating a soft landing for the three to five eggs that both male and female incubate and feed.

The birds feed by feel, searching with their long beaks in brackish and saltwater swamps for fish, frogs, baby alligators, and even snakes. When young are in the nest, the parents partly digest the food, then regurgitate it into the babies' beaks. Adults need about a pound of food daily, ranging as far as forty miles to find it. To raise a clutch of chicks, the stork must find and predigest more than four hundred pounds of food. Thus, the bird is known as the barometer of the health of a wetland area because, when water levels are too low, food is scarce and baby birds cannot thrive. Then populations dwindle, sending an early signal that the wetlands, and all the life they sustain, are threatened.

---

founder James Oglethorpe's original band. He settled here on the Isle of Hope, building his fort-home from 1739–1745 while doubling as constable, surveyor, and rum agent. The commander of a company of Royal Marines that defended the

Wood storks

Georgia coast against the Spanish, he was one of only a handful of early pioneers who survived the Low Country's hunger, Indian attacks, and fevers.

Today, only ruins of his five-room homestead remain, but an avenue of stately oaks survives. Explore a typical coastal forest and marvel at the wealth of flowering shrubs, pines, and oaks that greeted those hopeful first settlers.

Where: Wormsloe State Historic Site is ten miles southeast

of Savannah. Take US 516 east to Dererenne Avenue, then turn south (right) on Skidaway Road.
For more information: Wormsloe State Historic Site, 7601 Skidaway Road, Savannah, GA 31406; 912-352-2548.

Special note

For information on Wilderness Southeast, which offers scheduled and custom wilderness overnights on land, in canoes, or aboard sailboats in the barrier islands or Okefenokee, call 912-897-5108.

Further reading

Adventuring Along the Southeast Coast by John Bowen (Sierra Club Books) covers the coastal islands of North and South Carolina and Georgia.

Order maps or charts of the Georgia coast from Marine Sciences, Ecology Building, University of Georgia, Atlanta, GA 30602; 404-542-2112.

5

Plantation Trace

General Sherman's famous march to the sea began with the burning of Atlanta and continued with the torching of almost everything that stood in his path, but that is only half of the good news/bad news story. His route led southeast from Atlanta. Southwest Georgia was relatively untouched by the destruction brought by the War Between the States.

Today, this Southwest region, rich in antebellum treasures, is known as the Plantation Trace or the Plantation Crescent.

Largely recovered now from the devastating floods of 1994, it's a tourism bonanza of undiscovered woods and waters, unspoiled hamlets and timeless farms. As a bonus, the traveler sees a world of mid-nineteenth-century mansions in a setting of grand plantations, ancient oaks, formal gardens, and acres of native azaleas framed by fields that spill over with healthy crops of peanuts and canola.

It's a world apart from urban Georgia, a quiet retreat enjoyed as much by nature-loving Floridians and Alabamians as by the city folk of Atlanta.

The region is a rectangle bordered by the Chattahoochee River system on the west, the Florida border on the south, the Banks Lake National Wildlife Refuge on the east, and nothing more than a string of small towns in the north. Its center and largest city is Albany.

It should be noted that many acres in this region are privately owned or state-managed hunting preserves with some of the best duck, snipe, quail, deer, and turkey habitat in the country. For nonhunters, it means abundant sightings and photo ops.

The Chattahoochee flyway is also a bonanza for birdwatchers, who are never at a loss for sightings of nesting birds, migratory and occasional species, and accidental drop-ins that may include a loon, a red-billed tropic-bird, a white-winged owl, or a snow bunting.

In the highlands, hollows, and bogs, quiet observers may see marsh rabbits, shrews, armadillos, possums, loads of white-tail deer, raccoons, muskrats, field mice, skunks, river otters, and foxes. Moles drill through fields, leaving their telltale tunnels while bats can sometimes be seen almost smothering entire trees.

Admittedly, the chief natural wonder of this region—the mighty Chattahoochee itself—has been dammed, diked, dislocated, and distorted. Still, its waters have been gathered into lakes that have in turn been reclaimed by nature to create new homes for native flora and fauna.

Banks Lake National Wildlife Refuge

This glistening, 3,500-acre wildlife refuge looks as if it were created by Hollywood for a film about the Louisiana bayou country. The huge, flat, shallow lake is dotted with Spanish-moss-draped cypress trees, living and dead, that form a stark perch for buzzards, ospreys, grackles, and the occasional bald eagle. So famous is the bass fishing here that the refuge's potential for nature watching has almost been overlooked. In a canoe or kayak, you can skim for hours among trees and islands to look for freshwater turtles, water snakes, pelicans, anhingas, herons, ducks, and coots.

Where: Just west of Lakeland, off State 122.
Facilities: Marine and fishing supplies, boat rental, boardwalk/fishing pier.
For more information: Write U.S. Fish and Wildlife Service, attention (Banks Lake) National Wildlife Refuge, Richard R. Russell Federal Building, 75 Spring Street S.W., Atlanta, GA 30303; 404-331-0833.

Birdsong Nature Center

If you'll be in this area long enough, consider joining this nonprofit nature center to take advantage of the hours of enjoyment available to the bird-watching family. A tax-deductible,

Brown pelicans

one-year family membership can be purchased for the price of about four admissions.

Nature trails are open during limited hours and only to members and their guests. However, a gift shop and bird window are both open to the public. Sit for as long as you like watching for herons, anhingas, wood ducks, and a long list of songbirds.

Despite its limited public access, Birdsong is a naturalist's delight. Originally Birdsong Plantation, it was in the same family for four generations between the 1850s and the 1930s; the century-old barn is a favorite spot for nature programs. The present owners have turned the overworked farm fields into a skillfully managed habitat and haven for wildlife.

Set aside for the birds are 565 acres of varied habitats laced with twelve miles of trails. In the farmhouse, a bird window overlooks a unique viewing area. Volunteers are on hand to identify the birds and tell you about them. For members there is an extensive schedule of events: early morning and dusk birding, work days, nature photography workshops, birding by ear, talks and lectures. Bluebirds, which have disappeared from much of America's heartland, are seen in abundance here. Best of all is the zest of dedicated members and volunteers who make this a working, giving nature center.

Where: On Meridian Road south of Thomasville, four miles north of the Florida border. The bird window is open only three mornings a week. Admission. Call to verify times, which are subject to change.
Facilities: Gift shop, restrooms.
For more information: Route 3, Box 1077, Thomasville, GA 31792; 912-377-4408.

Chehaw Park

Lucky the citizens of Albany to have a park of this size and quality in the heart of town! The park covers eight hundred wooded acres filled with trails, bike paths, campsites, picnic grounds with grills, playgrounds, and a lake with boat rentals.

Each year, the hundred-acre Chehaw Wild Animal Park within this park attracts two hundred and fifty thousand visitors to see native and exotic animals roaming in open zones that have been landscaped to resemble their native environments in Africa, Australia, and the Americas. Stroll the easygoing boardwalks under dewy shade trees, to take nature as it comes. Some of the animals are in action in plain sight, but others snooze during the day or watch people warily from hiding places that can be spotted only by the practiced eye. Take your time, look carefully.

Where: Start at the Chamber of Commerce downtown on West Broad Avenue and go north on Jefferson Street, under the Liberty Expressway and right at the three-way stop onto State 91 to Philema Road. On your left, you'll see Lake Worth, which has a canoe trail and picnic pavilion. Watch for the park entrance on your left after the lake. Minimal fee. Closed Mondays, Christmas.
Facilities: Good walking trails and boardwalks, bicycle trails, camping, playground, food service, boating, restrooms, picnicking, nature programs, festivals, and special events, including the annual National Indian Festival. Held the third week in May, it's one of the nation's major Indian cultural events. During this time, Chehaw campsites are reserved for participating visitors; call to ask about camping nearby.
For more information: Chehaw Park, Philema Road, Albany, GA 31701; 912-430-5275.

Georgia Agrirama

Driving I-75 through south Georgia, try to imagine this region when it was a vast prairie covered in wiregrass and longleaf yellow pine. Cotton plantations sprang up in the rich soils to the east and west, but it wasn't until 1820 that the first sodbusters penetrated the prairie, cleared small plots of land, and began eking out crops to sustain their families.

It's this era that is re-created on the ninety-five acres of Georgia Agrirama, a living-history museum that portrays the era from 1870 to 1910. It's a chance to see the planting, growing, or harvesting of traditional crops using traditional methods, including syrup boiling, meat smoking, the grinding of meal and grits, cotton ginning, and the firing up of the turpentine still.

As a tourism attraction, it's natural and appealing. The costumed characters ready to answer your questions are mostly senior citizens who remember firsthand what it was to plow with mules and cook on woodstoves.

Where: Exit 20, I-75 at Tifton, a hundred and seventy-five miles south of Atlanta and sixty miles north of the Florida line. Admission.
Facilities: Snacks, restrooms, museum store with an excellent book selection, and picnic area. Wheelchair access is not good due to the authenticity of the buildings and grounds.
For more information: Georgia Agrirama, Box Q, Tifton, GA 31793; 912-386-3344.

Kolomoki Mounds State Historic Park

The plains are featureless, but suddenly they rise dramatically into a mound fifty-six feet high, topped by a plateau large enough for an entire tribe to meet for important ceremonies. It's obviously not a natural phenomenon, but today it must be counted among Georgia's natural wonders because it has been here since long before the first European explorers arrived. The largest mound here is also the largest mound east of the Mississippi River and is a National Historic Landmark.

In the museum, built over one of the burial mounds that

has been excavated, you'll see and hear the story of unknown peoples who, in the twelfth and thirteenth centuries, moved millions of basketloads of dirt and stone to create a massive ceremonial center.

Now a 1,293-acre park, Kolomoki has nature trails that thread through fields and forests roamed by quail, doves, deer, wild turkeys, and rabbits. In the wet thickets and meadows, look for vase flowers in early fall. In moist woodlands, find bluebells in spring and early summer.

Where: Six miles north of Blakely off US 27. The museum is open Tuesday to Saturday 9 A.M. to 5 P.M. and Sunday 2 to 5:30 P.M.
Facilities: Lake swimming, fishing, boating, camping, picnic areas, cabins, museum, outdoor displays, marked paths.
For more information: Kolomoki Mounds State Historic Park, Route 1 Box 114, Blakely, GA 37123; 912-723-5296.

Lake Seminole

One of several lakes in the Chattahoochee River system, Seminole is made special for many people by the presence here of one man: Jack Wingate. When a source suggested that we look him up at his Lunker Lodge near Bainbridge, we expected to find just another genial Georgia fish-camp operator whose talk focused more on bucketmouth bass than on a total picture of woods and water. Instead, we found an astute historian, author, naturalist, and native son who knows every season and secret of the area, based on explorations since his boyhood.

The 37,500-acre natural lake, with two hundred and fifty miles of meandering shoreline in Georgia's subtropic lowlands, is formed by the confluence of the Chattahoochee and Flint Rivers. The Flint, called that for good reason, continues to be a happy hunting ground for old arrowheads and other

Indian artifacts. Artifacts found in the area include fossils fifteen thousand years old, Civil War relics, and debris left by early twentieth-century steamboat traffic.

Long before Hernando de Soto explored Decatur County, Indians roamed the bluffs overlooking the Flint. As late as 1765, the area now known as Bainbridge was an Indian village called Pucknawhitla. A bloody Indian massacre brought in federal troops under the command of Generals Andrew Jackson and Zachary Taylor. Fort Scott was established near the lake; Camp Recovery was built to shelter sick and injured soldiers.

After a malaria epidemic in 1821, the camp was abandoned, but Wingate and other local historians have mapped and marked dozens of significant sites. Ask for a self-guided driving-tour map. Tour by water, too, exploring both lake and river aboard a rental boat. Watch the banks for bird, small mammals, the occasional deer, and a cross section of native trees, shrubs, vines, and wildflowers.

At Wingate's Lunker Lodge, order the chicken dinner for an unpretentious, tasty, farmhand meal at very modest prices. Take time to look around. Wingate's collection of Indian relics is authentic and superb. In one corner under a pile of fishing magazines, you'll find some of his excellent self-published books for sale. In another corner, look for the shelves of homemade jellies and relishes prepared by local folk and sold here.

One interesting geological note: Decatur County is the nation's leading producer of fuller's earth, a special clay that has been mined commercially here since the early 1900s. Its early uses were for bleaching petroleum and cleaning wool; today, it is used in many ways, including the making of cat litter.

Where: Jack Wingate's Lunker Lodge is south of Bainbridge

on State 97. The Seminole state park is sixteen miles south of Donalsville on State 39.
Facilities: Jack Wingate's Lunker Lodge offers camping, boats, guides, fishing supplies, meals, and lodgings. Lake Seminole State Park has camping, cottages, picnic sites and shelters, boating, launch ramps, swimming, and nature trails.
For more information: Jack Wingate's Lunker Lodge, Route 1, Box 3311, Bainbridge, GA 31717; 912-246-0658.

Lake Seminole State Park, Route 2, Donalsville, GA 31745; 912-861-3137.

Lake Walter F. George

George T. Bagby State Park covers three hundred acres on the shore of the 48,000-acre Lake Walter F. George, created by a massive dam that is also open to the public. Come to stay in the comfortable lodge or one of the enormously popular cottages that overlook the lake. The restaurant in the lodge is a local favorite or take your choice of shaded or sunny picnic tables around the park.

Along the one-and-one-tenth-mile hiking trail, you'll pass willow and water oak, shortleaf and loblolly pine, dogwood, black cherry, sweetgum, mockernut hickory, magnolia, maple, wax myrtle, elm, and many more native trees. Look carefully and you'll see a gopher-tortoise den and a red-fox den with several entrances. Watch out for the sumac. It's a year-round show of greenery, red berry clusters, and turning leaves, but it causes an allergic reaction in some people.

Where: North of Fort Gaines three miles, off State 39; call 312-768-2571.
Facilities: Reservations for the lodge and cottages are essential. Restaurant, marina with docks, boat launch, fuel and marine supplies, picnic sites, picnic shelters that are wheelchair accessible, swimming beach.

Dogwood

For more information: George T. Bagby State Park and Lodge, Route 1, Box 201, Fort Gaines, GA 31751; 912-768-2571.

Cotton Hill Park, operated by the U.S. Army Corps of Engineers on a peninsula formed by the lake and Sandy Creek,

is one of the most scenic, clean, spacious, and comfortable campgrounds in the state. More than a hundred waterfront sites have electric and water hookups, grills, metal fire pits, picnic tables, and fish-cleaning tables. Most people just pull their boats up on the shore at their own campsites. For tent campers, there are sites handy to toilet and shower facilities.
For more information: U.S. Army Corps of Engineers, 77 Forsyth Street S.W., Room 313, Atlanta, GA 30335; 404-331-6746. Locally, call 912-768-3061.

Paradise Park

In the heart of the charming old city of Thomasville, where actress Joanne Woodward grew up and Jacqueline Kennedy came to find quiet solace after JFK's assassination, this eighteen-acre jewel on South Broad Street is green with pines all year and blooms in season with dogwood, roses, azaleas, and crape myrtle. Photography is especially good in early morning and late afternoon, when low sun backlights the Spanish moss to create silvery billows among the trees.

Where: Downtown on Broad Street, just south of the junction of Business 19 and Business 84. Open daylight hours free.
For more information: Thomasville Tourism Authority, Box 1540, Thomasville, GA 31799; 912-225-5222.

Pebble Hill Plantation

Imagine strolling the grounds of the mythical Tara under sheltering live oaks on miles of azalea-lined paths. Although the mansion is the center of attention here, the nature lover can buy a ticket to the grounds only and spend an entire day marveling at the gardens and paths, cataloging abundant bird life.

The present mansion dates only to the 1930s, but it's typical of the extravagant plantations that for years have hosted quail hunters who come from all over the world (including the

White House and Buckingham Palace) for an interlude of hunt breakfasts, luxury living, blueblood horses, good bourbon, and shooting sports.

Because hunting and the opulent life that goes with it are so important a part of the culture of Georgia, a house tour makes an interesting side trip.

Where: On US 319, five miles south of Thomasville and twenty miles north of Tallahassee, Florida. Call 912-226-2344. Grounds are open Tuesday to Saturday 10 A.M. to 5 P.M., Sunday 1 to 5 P.M. Admission.
Facilities: Picnic areas, gift shop, restrooms. Visitors to the grounds are free to tour outbuildings, including barns, the log-cabin schoolhouse, stables, a carriage house, Noah's Ark (a former playhouse now filled with paintings of animals), the kennels, and an old cemetery. Note that mansion tours are at additional cost and are closed to children younger than first graders.

Radium Springs, Albany

Radium Springs is the state's largest natural spring and one of the Seven Wonders of Georgia. Swim in cold water as clear as a martini and stroll through moist woodlands past gazebos and park benches.

In the 1920s, the springs site was chosen for the building of a lavish casino complex that for years was the gathering place of the swank, naughty set who continued to drink and gamble during the Prohibition years. The grandly pillared casino burned in the early 1980s but was rebuilt and reopened in the 1990s.

Once again, the radiant springs are the playground, swimming paradise, and a place for smart-set meeting and dining. The Flint River often floods in the spring, inundating the springs and covering the surrounding park. During flood conditions, call ahead.

Where: From downtown Albany, go east on Oglethorpe Boulevard, then south on Radium Springs Road.
Note: Older guidebooks refer to sand dunes on East Oglethorpe, which were a geological phenomenon thought to have been the original beaches of the Gulf of Mexico. These dunes have largely disappeared under development and are, unfortunately, no longer a significant natural wonder.
Facilities: Radium Springs has bathhouses, swimming, food service, and picnicking. Call ahead; facilities vary seasonally.
For more information: Radium Springs, 2500 Radium Springs Road, Albany, GA 31705; call Albany Convention and Visitors Bureau, 912-434-8700.

Ramona's Garden

The Dill House in Fort Gaines is a dream-come-true story that belongs in the historian's book of bed and breakfasts. Here, however, we must simply note the magical transformation that innkeeper Ramona Kurland has wrought on the intimidating tangle that had replaced the property's once-grand gardens. The house itself has been largely restored by Ramona and her husband, Phillip. It's a showplace of oak floors and rare wainscoting, with half a dozen big, airy rooms for overnight guests.

In the tranquil grounds, Ramona planted seventy rose bushes to accent some two thousand native azaleas and camellias. Even if you're not staying here, stop to shop the gift shop and to stroll garden paths past the fishpond, wishing well, and year-round blooms.

Take the self-guided walking tour around Fort Gaines, where geological history goes back some seventy million years and where mountain laurel, native to north Georgia, grows side by side with maidenhair fern, which is native to Florida.

Where: Dill House, 102 South Washington Street, Fort Gaines, GA 31751; 912-768-2338.
Facilities: Gift shop, bed and breakfast, garden.

Reed Bingham State Park

It wasn't until the 1950s that this park came into being. A dam built across Little River created a lake, but the dam broke in 1966, and the present lake didn't take shape until the 1970s. Still, Reed Bingham State Park is laced with short, but significant, trails through typical coastal-plains terrain.

Old fields in the first stages of their return to nature shelter squirrels and possums, songbirds and a growing population of game birds. Ramble through the bay swamp, which looks more like a scrub thicket because of the many sprouts from old stumps. Wander into the pine flatwoods and look for quail and rabbits and through the pitcher-plant savannah to see the type of plant life that once covered so much of the coastal plain. Look closely at the many insectivorous plants and watch as they snare and digest bugs. Rare plants growing here include long-leafed and round-leafed sundew, many butterworts, and both hooded and trumpet pitcher plants.

Longleaf pines, the trees once tapped for turpentine and today a valuable source of wood pulp, prevail along the Upland Pine Woods Trail. Plants typical of the driest sand-ridge terrain can be seen along the Turkey Oak Pine Woods Trail. This is also the best spot to look for gopher tortoise and the endangered indigo snake.

Because the Little River floods periodically, creating swampland along its sides, this area is a good place to see lush climbing plants, including wild muscadines. Watch out for poison ivy, which thrives in this environment. Walk quietly in the flood-plain areas in hopes of surprising a deer on its way to get a drink in the river or swamp.

The spring-fed freshwater pond will have waterlilies in bloom if you're lucky. Follow what is called the Birdwalk

Wood duck

through more swampland and watch for wood ducks in large dead trees, where they nest. They're year-round residents. The land rises slightly to form a cypress-gum swamp. You'll see a few young cypresses, but mostly it's an area of black gums ringed with ferns.

In winter, the barren trees of this park turn inky with hundreds of roosting buzzards. It's worth a trip during the off-season just to see them.

The trails are short, ranging from three-tenths to nine-tenths of a mile, but can be turned into a day-long backpack adventure if you plan a walk through all the connecting loops.

Where: Reed Bingham State Park is six miles west of Adel on State 37. Take exit 10 off I-75.
Facilities: Camping, picnic sites and shelters, boating, fishing, swimming beach, nature/hiking trails.

ABOUT MAYHAWS

A tart, red-tinged yellow fruit that grows wild on trees that live in shallow water, mayhaws might be compared to cranberries for size and taste or to crab apples for the delicate jelly they make. To get a taste of this delightful folk product, visit Wilkins' I.G.A. supermarket on West Main Street in Colquitt, where there's usually a pot of mayhaws simmering on the back of the stove in the deli.

Locals gather mayhaw in season using boats, boots, and patience. They sell them by the quart to the I.G.A., where they are stored in the freezer until needed. The jelly is sold from the shelf like any other supermarket product, a wonderful souvenir find for the traveler. Mayhaw jelly and products starring Vidalia onions are also made and sold at the Mayhaw Tree, 560 East Main Street. The I.G.A. Deli's phone number is 912-758-2898; the Mayhaw Tree's is 800-677-3227.

THE LOWDOWN ON LIME SINKS

You'll hear the term lime sink used often in southern Georgia, not only to describe a geological feature but also in a botanical context (ideal for growing mayhaws) and an angling context (great honey holes for fishing). Formed by the collapse of underlying limestone caverns, these sinks, most of them small and shallow, fill with water. Some appear as pools or swamps in fields or woodland; others are below lake level and are sought out by fishermen with echo sounders. Twin lime sinks in Albany are used as natural tunnels. Through a closed cave chimney, engineers are able to delve thirty feet below Hugh Mills Stadium to check periodically for structural stability.

For more information: Route 2, Box 394 B-1, Adel, GA 31620; 912-896-3551.

Thomasville Big Oak

For longer than Thomasville has been a settlement, this giant oak tree has been a landmark. Standing there at the corner of Monroe and Crawford Streets, it is sixty-eight feet high, has a limb spread of a hundred and sixty-two feet, and is twenty-four feet in circumference.

Facilities: None.
For more information: Destination Thomasville, Box 1540, Thomasville, GA 31799; 912-225-5222.

6

Presidential Pathways

Two presidents are associated with the portion of west central Georgia that includes Columbus, Callaway Gardens, and the Andersonville Trail. Probably the better known is Jimmy Carter, the peanut farmer from Plains. Less well known to younger people is Franklin D. Roosevelt, who, crippled from polio, came to Warm Springs for rest and treatment in the warm, naturally healing waters.

On the rolling plains with their rich, red soil, agriculture is king. Along the rivers, woodlands, and high ridges, recreation rules. The western border of this fortunate region is the Chattahoochee River system.

Blanton Creek Park

Land owned by Georgia Power on Lake Harding has been turned into a public recreation area. Come for the camping, boating, fishing, and breezy picnics along the water.

Where: Lick Skillet Road at Lake Harding; 706-643-7737.
Facilities: Boat launch, tent and RV camping, picnicking, playground, rest rooms.
For more information: Georgia Power Company, Land Department, 1516 Barlett's Ferry Road, Fortson, GA 31808; 706-643-7737.

Callaway Gardens and the Pine Mountain Trail

More than a botanical showplace, Callaway Gardens is one of America's largest resorts. The golf greens, woodlands, lakes, and gardens spread over 14,000 acres of what was once a sea of cotton surrounding Pine Mountain, which stretches for a hundred and ten miles from Barnesville into Alabama. Aeons ago, this was a sea bottom that hardened to quartzite, which in turn crumpled and cracked during the Paleozoic Period.

Over millennia, soils grew thick and rich, but in only a century of cotton growing they were left lifeless and exhausted. The Callaways, searching for a future for this depleted land, reclaimed and replanted and turned it into a verdant showplace. Appropriately, their money put back into the soil what they and their cotton mills had taken away. They created not only beauty but a new, intelligent land-management style that continues to give back with each passing year.

By happy coincidence, they discovered early that the native Prunifolia Azalea, which was almost extinct, still clung to life in scattered patches here. Nurtured and propagated, it now flourishes in its homeland, blooming in June and July. Through the summer, this is also the place to see pinckneya (fever tree), whose brilliant bloom looks much like the winter-blooming poinsettia.

In a 7,000-square-foot conservatory, more than fifty species of butterflies flutter by. It's a destination in itself, well worth half a day. Outdoors, you can ramble for hours through one of the world's largest botanical gardens. In the horticultural center, more than eighteen major floral shows are held each year. Jewell Callaway's vegetable garden covers seven and a half acres of perfectly tended fruits, vegetables, and herbs typical of species that thrive at this latitude.

Of all the plantings, the Azalea Trail is the most famous. Experience it March through May. As it fades in late spring, the Rhododendron Trail takes the spotlight. Equally dazzling are the Laurel Springs Trail, best when the mountain laurels are in bloom in spring, and the Wildflower Trail, from spring through fall. In winter, red berries and brilliant camellias line the Holly Trail.

Where: On US 27 in Pine Mountain, seventy miles south of Atlanta and thirty miles north of Columbus. The resort is open all year. Gardens are best from March through early November.
Facilities: Four golf courses, swimming, tennis on hard and soft courts, horticultural center, water-skiing, boating, racquet ball, fine dining, cottages, villas, inn, shops, hunting preserve, swimming beach, playgrounds, planned recreation programs in summer.
For more information: Callaway Gardens, Pine Mountain, GA 31822 2000; 800-282-8181.

Pine Mountain Trail starts at the scenic overlook parking lot at Callaway Gardens and winds for twenty-three miles past buzzard nests and bear grass, through native azalea and seas of rhododendron along creeks with waterfalls and beaver ponds. Rocky, soil-poor hillsides are covered with dwarf oak and hawthorn. For local information, ask at the Country Store or at FDR State Park. The trail ends at the TV tower on Georgia 85 West.

Columbus Riverwalk

Although it's in the heart of a teeming city, the promenade that follows the Chattahoochee River in downtown Columbus is a triumph of urban renewal. Walk or jog this pathway, which will eventually be part of a forty-mile biking and jogging network through the city.

Where: The riverwalk begins at Dilligham Street Bridge, which connects Columbus with Phenix City, Alabama.
For more information: Convention and Visitors Bureau, 801 Front Avenue, Columbus, GA 31902; 706-3221613 or 800-999-1613.

Franklin D. Roosevelt State Park

Named for the president who came to nearby Warm Springs for treatment after he was stricken with polio in 1921, this 10,000-acre park has a rustic, 1930s air. The route, which is near his Little White House and was one of FDR's favorite rides, is a pretty one. Even if you don't have time to stop, drive this way for the scenery. At Dowdell's Knob, FDR's preferred picnic site, stop for a panoramic view of the valley below. FDR's grill, now a monument, remains.

Where: West of Warm Springs at 2970 State 190, east of Pine Mountain, GA 31822; 706-663-4858. Open 7 A.M. to 10 P.M. Park office, 8 A.M. to 5 P.M. Little White House, 706-655-3511, open 9 A.M. to 5 P.M. daily except Thanksgiving and Christmas.
Facilities: Thirty miles of hiking trails, including a twenty-three-mile backpacking trail, cabins, tent and RV campsites with hookups, spring-fed pool, twelve-minute movie about FDR, museum of Roosevelt memorabilia, lakes, fishing, picnicking. Reservations advised for guided horseback rides by the hour, half day, or overnight. For reservations, 706-628-4533.

Georgia Veterans Memorial State Park

This 1,322-acre park is built around a theme other than nature, but there is plenty here for boaters, fishermen, and campers. Indoor and outdoor museums honor Georgia's veterans with exhibits from wars starting with the French and Indian wars of the eighteenth century and going through Vietnam. It's an appropriate spot in which to remember veterans because Cordele is the starting point for driving the eighty-five-mile Andersonville Trail. In the notorious Confederate prison camp at Andersonville, 12,900 Union prisoners died of starvation, disease, exposure, and neglect. It's now a National Historic Site.

Boat, fish, or water-ski on scenic Lake Blackshear, which covers seven thousand acres. Picnic, fly model airplanes in a special paved flying area, play the eighteen-hole golf course, or swim in the pool or lake.

Where: Nine miles west of I-75 exit 33, near Cordele on US 280.
For more information: Georgia Veterans Memorial State Park, 2459-A US Highway 280 West, Cordele, GA 31015; 912-276-2371. Golf course, 912-276-2377.
Facilities: Picnic areas, golf, camping, war museums, fishing, boating, water-skiing, boat launch, swimming pool, beach.

Lake Walter F. George

Read more about this miles-long lake in the Chattahoochee River system in the Plantation Trace section. It extends from Florence to Fort Gaines and is a major recreation resource for Georgians and Alabamians. Fishing is one of the chief attractions, but it's also a major bird-watching center all year and especially during spring and fall migrations.

Also in the park is Kirbo Interpretive Center, which

houses local artifacts and nature exhibits. Through the Interpretive Center, arrange a guided walking tour of the Rood Creek Indian Mounds.

Where: On State 39C at the lake, sixteen miles west of Lumpkin.
Facilities: Tent and RV camping, swimming pool, tennis courts, marina, rental cottages, lighted fishing pier, miniature golf.
For more information: Florence Marina State Park, Route 1, Box 36, Omaha, GA 31821; 706-838-6870.

Pine Mountain Wild Animal Park

Familiar and exotic animals from seven continents appear to roam freely through five hundred green and scenic acres. Visit the petting zoo and Old McDonald's Farm, laugh at the monkeys, and see the serpentarium and alligator pit. Walk the park, drive around, or take the bus tour.

Where: From Atlanta, take I-85 south to exit 14, go left on US 27 for seven miles, then right on Oak Grove Road. Admission. Open every day except Christmas, Thanksgiving, and New Year's Day from 10 A.M. until one hour before sunset.
Facilities: Gift shop, restaurant, snack bar, picnic area, and kennel (pets are not allowed in the park, nor should they be left in a car or RV in warm weather).
For more information: Pine Mountain Wild Animal Park, 1300 Oak Grove Road, Pine Mountain, GA 31822; 706-663-8744.

Providence Canyon State Conservation Park

The Chattahoochee River has bitten through layer after layer of soils here, creating rainbows of color along canyon cliffs and carving tall sculptures in the limestone. The remaining topsoil is clay, once the floor of an ocean. Come to hike the trails—there's an easy one and a rugged one—to see wild plum-leaf azalea in early summer and a wildflower show that lasts well into the fall.

Where: Seven miles west of Lumpkin via State 39C.
Facilities: Camping,picnic shelters, nature trails, interpretive center. Limited handicap access.
For more information: Providence Canyon State Park, Route 1 Box 158, Lumpkin, GA 31815; 706-838-6202.

Shenandoah Environment and Education Center

If you're in the Newnan area, schedule a brief stop at this education center for a look at displays describing the ecology of the area. It's a local center, used primarily for school groups, but the public is welcome.

Where: In the Shenandoah Industrial Park at exit 9 off I-85.
Facilities: Educational displays, restrooms.
For more information: Shenandoah Environment and Education Center, 7 Solar Circle, Newnan, GA 30264; 800-342-6547. Open weekdays 8 a.m to 5 P.M. free.

Sprewell Bluff

This high bluff overlooking the Flint River is a good place to stop for photographs, a tailgate lunch, and perhaps a hike down to the river to wet a line.

Where: Nine miles west of Thomaston off State 74 West.
For more information: Chamber of Commerce, 201 South Center Street, Thomaston, GA 30286; 706-647-1703. For information on guided camping and canoeing excursions on the Flint River, call 706-647-2633.

7

Atlanta and the Historic Heartland

Georgia state tourism divides this area into two portions, Metro Atlanta and Historic Heartland, but we're carving it out as one region at the center of the Peachtree State. Unlike all the other regions, which end at a state border, this one is entirely surrounded by other Georgia regions.

Our Georgia heartland starts in the foothills and spreads out from the great, pulsing city to unspoiled farmlands to the south and foothills to the north. For nature lovers, it offers the most variety and also the most easy access from the city.

Atlanta Botanical Garden

Plan at least half a day for the safari that takes you from a steamy jungle into a desert, past misty waterfalls, and into the fragrant, outdoor piedmont. The conservatory alone is a 16,000-square-foot garden for tropical, desert, and endangered plants. Outdoors, walk through fifteen acres of hardwoods and see special gardens of roses, vegetables, herbs, native perennials, and a serene, uncrowded Japanese garden.

Where: Piedmont Road at The Prado between 14th Street and Monroe Drive.
Facilities: Restrooms, gift shop. Note: strollers are permitted outdoors but not in the conservatory.
For more information: Atlanta Botanical Garden, Box 77246, Atlanta, GA 30357. Call 404-876-5858 for a twenty-four-hour events line. Admission.

Atlanta History Center

Set among thirty-two acres of formal and wild gardens filled with flowers and foliage are homes and exhibits from the city's past, from the simple Tullie Smith Farm, circa 1840, to the architecturally important Swan House, built in 1928. Also in the complex are a library, museum shop, café, and outbuildings where crafters are at work. Don't get so caught up in the house tours and museum that you neglect the natural wonders of this urban oasis.

Where: 130 East Paces Ferry Road, Atlanta, GA 30305; 404-814-4000. Admission is charged over age six. Call for hours, which vary seasonally.
Facilities: Café, restrooms, shop, library, house tours, crafts.

Bo Ginn National Fish Hatchery and Aquarium

Many of Georgia's lakes and streams are stocked with hatchery-raised fish from resources like this one. Take an educational tour to see how fingerlings are raised for release in the wild. In the twenty-six aquariums, you can study the many species of fish raised here in their various stages of development.

Where: On US 25, five miles north of Millen. Open daily 9 A.M. to 4 P.M. Free.
For more information: Augusta Welcome Center, 8th at Reynolds, Augusta, GA 30913. Hatchery, 912-982-1700.

Brown's Mount, Macon

At the fall line where the piedmont overlaps the coastal plain, a rise now called Brown's Mount heaved up untold aeons ago. It has known human habitation for probably twelve thousand years and still has remnants of a pre-Columbian rock wall and cistern that was described in 1849 by an early historian. Today, the site is held in trust by the Museum of Arts and Sciences, which is developing educational, archaeological, historical, and preservation programs.

Today's second-growth pines succeed centuries of timbering, farming, grazing, and retimbering, so it's a good study in the changing role of nature and humankind in this area. The site adjoins the 6,500-acre Bond Swamp National Wildlife Refuge, which is also accessed through the museum.

Where: The Museum of Arts and Sciences, which includes the Mark Smith Planetarium, is at 4182 Forsyth Road, Macon, GA 31210. Hours at different museum facilities vary, so call ahead. Admission.
Facilities: At the museum are nature trails, live animals, science exhibits, and an observatory. Access for the mobility impaired is limited; check ahead. Call 912-477-3232 for information about programs at Brown's Mount or the wildlife refuge.

Chattahoochee Nature Center

On the banks of the Chattahoochee River, walk nature trails and a boardwalk and visit the Birds of Prey Rehabilitation Center, where injured birds are being prepared to re-enter their natural environment.

Wandering the wetlands area, look for marsh rabbits, muskrats, and beavers and listen for the call of red-winged blackbirds. Cattails galore and fringes of buttonbush are part of nature's water filter, cleansing water before it flows into the river. Within the shelter of the bullrushes are families of blackbirds, catbirds, ducks, wrens, and rails. Beyond them, look for marsh feeders such as great-blue herons, green-backed herons, and belted kingfishers.

In season, joe pyeweed, jewelweed, cardinal flowers, and tulip poplar bloom. On the high ground, oaks, hickories, and other hardwoods form a canopy for dogwood and sour-wood. Moss and lichen cling to riverside rocks, natural hiding holes for skinks, moles, mice, and shrews. In the bogs, you'll see salamanders, box turtles, and frogs.

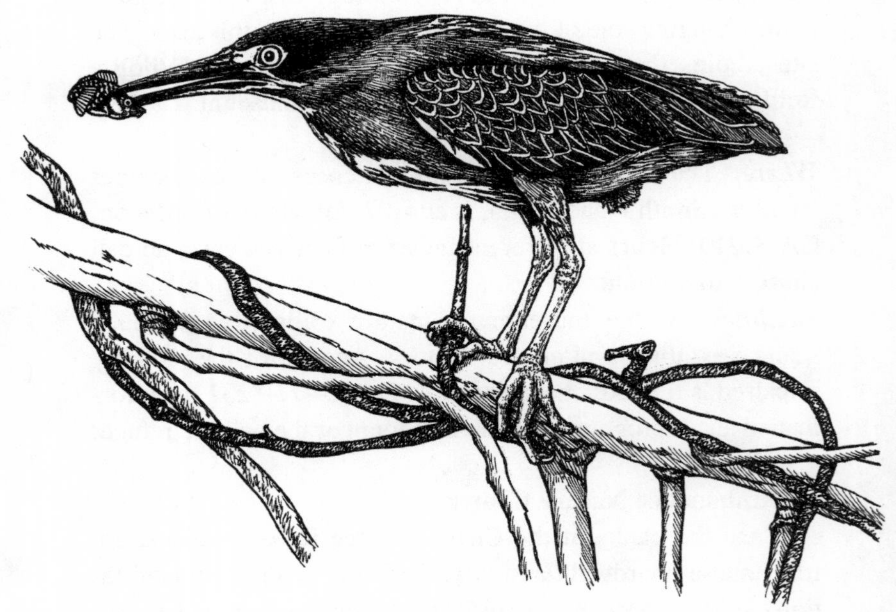

Green-backed heron

Only a chimney remains from an old house (probably post-World War II), but it too is alive with nature: bats, lizards, toads, and chimney swifts. Take to the trails on quiet weekends or be here during special events. This is a busy, breathing nature center for families who like a structured approach and well-staged events that utilize the center's natural environment to the fullest.

Where: Chattahoochee Nature Center, 9135 Willeo Road, Roswell, GA 30075; 404-992-2055. From downtown Atlanta or I-285, go north on Roswell Road, take the first left (Azalea Drive) after crossing the Chattahoochee River. Turn left on Willeo Road, then go half a mile. The center is on your right. From Marietta and the west, take Marietta Highway (State 120) east toward Roswell. Cross Johnson Ferry Road, then go four miles to Willeo Road, right at the traffic light, and one mile to the Center on your right. Open Monday-Saturday 9 A.M. to 5 P.M., Sunday noon to 5 P.M. Guided walks weekends at 1 and 3 P.M. Closed Thanksgiving, Christmas, New Year's Day. Admission.
Facilities: Nature store, naturalist-led walks, camping and canoe field trips, special events tied to seasons. Nature trails, restrooms. The center is between two parks that are part of the Chattahoochee River National Recreation Area listed below. Both have picnic areas; a launch ramp is found just north of the center.

Chattahoochee National Recreation Area

The mighty Chattahoochee River starts as meager creeks in the mountains of northern Georgia and ends four hundred and thirty-six miles later when it meets the Flint River at Lake Seminole in southwest Georgia. This section of the river is a forty-eight-mile series of parklands that follows the Chattahoochee River from Lake Sidney Lanier to Atlanta. Along its swift-flowing course, you'll find frequent launch points, picnic and parking areas, ranger stations, hiking trails, and points of interest; the waters themselves range from a serene Class I to as frisky as Class III.

Fabled for rainbow- and brown-trout fishing, this stretch of the river also hosts bream, catfish, and other species. If you fish, get a Georgia license and review river regulations regarding limits, seasons, locales, and artificial lures. Live bait may not be used here.

Floating the Chattahoochee on rafts is a local passion, although some prefer a faster passage by canoe or kayak. The longest leg, from Buford Dam to Abbotts Bridge, is thirteen miles and takes six to eight hours in a canoe or nine to ten hours by raft. Another long leg, Jones Bridge to Chattahoochee River Park, is twelve miles. Other legs range from two to four miles.

In burrows along the banks, the vigilant passerby will see beaver and muskrat burrows and perhaps the occasional fox or raccoon. Chipmunks, squirrels, and rabbits are quite at home, while turtles bask on sunny logs and butterflies flit brightly along banks abloom with dogwood, redbud, asters, and wild violets. In fall, red is the key color thanks to sumac and cardinal flowers.

For a quick hike of the best wildflowers, take the Paces Mill Loop Trail. In springtime, it's bright with several types of wild orchids, mayapple, fire pink, three kinds of trilliums, and two types of toothwort.

Where: Take I-285 in Atlanta to exit 41 (US 41), pass the Galleria Mall, and turn left. When you reach the river, turn right into the entrance nearest the Paces Mill Loop Trail.
Facilities: Park units along the river have hiking trails, picnic tables, grills, trash containers, and open meadows for playing. Trails in the Palisades Unit lead to views of the river gorge,

then wind down through woodlands to the river with its rock outcroppings and sandy beaches. In the Sope Creek and Vickery Creek units, trails lead through rolling hills past old homesteads and mills. Trails in Cochran Shoals, Johnson Ferry, and Gold Branch abound in marsh life. At Cochran, a fitness trail with twenty-two stations is three miles long. It's also accessible to wheelchairs and bicycles. Paces Mill, Island Ford, and Jones Bridge areas offer a good view of white-water shoals. The Chattahoochee Nature Center listed above is between the Vickery Creek and Gold Branch units. Both have picnic areas.

For more information: Write the Park Superintendent, Chattahoochee National Recreation Area, 1978 Island Fort Parkway, Dunwoody, GA 30350; 404-394-7912, for a map showing the entire system with all its access points and parks.

Dauset Trails Nature Center

Roam one thousand natural acres only a few miles off I-75 in an area known for its wildflowers. A nice side trip from High Falls State Park, the center has six miles of hiking trails, plant and tree identification, wildflower programs, and ecology education.

Where: On Mt. Vernon Road, off State 42. Call 404-775-6798.

Facilities: Trails, nature programs, restrooms.

For more information: Butts County Chamber of Commerce, 143 East College Street, Jackson, GA 30223; 404-775-4839.

Fernbank Science Center

Fernbank Science Center consists of one of the nation's largest planetariums, Georgia's first IMAX theater, a greenhouse, and botanical gardens. In its fifteen galleries, follow the natural chronology of the state from the beginning of time to the present. Don't miss the seashell collection and the dinosaur gallery.

The adjacent sixty-five-acre Fernbank Forest, greenhouse, and gardens are open to all visitors, free. Pathways are paved and some are adapted for the physically impaired. The forest is of special interest because, protected since 1939, it remains almost as it was when it was the home of the Creek Indians two centuries ago. It's said to be the only remaining stand of virgin forest in the Appalachian Piedmont.

Where: 156 Heaton Park Drive N.E., Atlanta, GA 30307.
Facilities: Admission is charged to the Science Center. Open Monday 8:30 A.M. to 5 P.M., Tuesday to Friday 8:30 A.M. to 10 P.M., Saturday 10 A.M. to 5 P.M. and Sun. 1 to 5 P.M. Hours vary for some programs and facilities. Some features are closed to very young children. Call ahead.
For more information: Call 404-378-4211.

Also maintained by Fernbank is the Cator Woolford Memorial Garden at 1815 Ponce de Leon Avenue N.E., near Olmsted Parks. Once part of a sprawling estate, these sunken gardens, which are at their best during azalea and dogwood bloom in spring, are a recreation area for patients of the Cerebral Palsy Center, but the public is also welcome. Open daylight hours. No facilities.

Fernbank Museum of Natural History

The story of the earth is told here in microcosm. Two major environments are aimed at children: Georgia Adventure, for ages six to ten, and Fantasy Forest, for ages three to five. Take in a show at the IMAX theater. There's a museum shop and a dining area.

Where: 767 Clifton Road, Atlanta, GA 30307; 404-378-0127.

Fort Yargo State Park

The fort was built in the 1790s to withstand Indian attacks, and now the original four blockhouses have been replicated. The park covers 1,850 acres of lakefront meadows between Atlanta and Athens. The park offers typical state park facilities plus an entire recreation area that is wheelchair accessible. It includes cottages, food service, and picnic and fishing areas.

Where: One mile south of Winder on State 81. Mailing address: Fort Yargo State Park, Box 764, Winder, GA 30680.
Facilities: Tent and trailer camping, miniature golf, tennis courts, nature trail, canoe and boat rental, picnic shelters, accessible area for persons with handicaps.
For more information: Call 404-867-3489.

Hard Labor Creek State Park

Hard Labor Creek, probably named by slaves who once tilled these fields, cuts through this 5,805-acre state park and joins the Apalachee River twenty-five miles downstream. It's best known for its snazzy, eighteen-hole golf course but the motivated nature lover can bypass the crowds. Bring your own horse to ride the fifteen-mile bridle trail or strike out on two and a half miles of trails through gentle hills and a fledgling forest.

Where: North of I-20. Take exit 49 into Rutledge, then go two miles on Fairplay Road to the park.
Facilities: Golf course with pro shop, rental carts, driving range; boat rentals, trails, tent and trailer camping, rental cottages, picnic shelters, swimming beach with bathhouse.
For more information: Hard Labor Creek State Park, Box 27, Rutledge, GA 30663; 706-557-3001.

High Falls State Park

Rushing waters cascading over rocks sang a siren song to industrial developers of the early nineteenth century, who needed the waters of the Towaliga River to run their mills. A thriving settlement here included a hotel, blacksmith shop, shoe factory, cotton gin, gristmill, and shops, but when the railroad passed it by, the town withered. Today, only the ghosts remain along hiking trails that are marked for their historic and natural features. Come in March when the forsythia is in bloom.

Where: One and eight-tenths miles east of I-75 exit 65 at High Falls Road.
Facilities: Tent and trailer camping, lake, miniature golf, swimming pool, interpretive trails, waterfall.
For more information: High Falls State Park, Route 5, Box 202-A, Jackson, GA 30233; 912-994-5080.

Indian Springs

The healing waters of this ancient spring still bring faithful followers here daily to fill their canteens and jerry cans. The old Indian Springs Hotel, which was built in 1823 by Chief William McIntosh of the Lower Creek Nation, is a lively center of local life and special events May through early October. Don't miss the garden, which has been faithfully restored as a nineteenth-century rose, flower, and herb garden. Its promoters claim it is the only truly authentic such garden in the southeast.

Where: Four miles southeast of Jackson on State 42.
Facilities: Camping, playground, hotel.
For more information: Indian Spring State Park, Route 1, Box 439, Indian Springs, GA 30216; 770-775-7241; hotel, 770-775-6734.

Lake Oconee

Like so many of Georgia's lakes, this one was not formed by nature but has settled into the natural scheme of things as shoreline growths mature. Created by the damming of the Oconee River, the 19,000-acre lake has almost four hundred miles of meandering shoreline where you can puddle about in a small boat to look for amphibians, small animals, wild birds, and a profusion of native trees.

Where: East of Madison off I-20.
Facilities: Beach, boating, marina, picnic tables, camping.
For more information: Convention and Visitors Bureau, 115 East Jefferson Street, Madison, GA 30650; 706-342-4454. Lake telephone, 706-485-8704.

Mockingbird

Lake Tobesofkee

Crowded on weekends with campers and boaters, this 1,750-acre lake still offers miles of secluded shoreline where nature observers spot goldfinches, cardinals, warblers, mockingbirds, and cedar waxwings among the sweetgum and oaks. Walk the park's nature trails to look for wild iris, ladies tresses, lizard's tail, sorrel, and poke.

Where: Three miles west of Macon, off the Thomaston Road exit of I-475.
Facilities: Tent and trailer camping, playground, swimming, beaches, boating, launch ramp, docks, ball diamond, tennis court, picnic tables, nature trails.
For more information: Convention and Visitors Bureau, Box 6354, Macon, GA 31201; 912-743-3401. Park number, 912-474-8770.

Lockerly Arboretum

One forty-seven-acre park paradise seems to sum up many of the natural wonders of Georgia, both native and introduced. The grounds of Lockerly Arboretum radiate from regal Lockerly Hall, a Greek Revival temple-style house that was built in the mid-nineteenth century and is not open to the public. Take a walking or driving tour through worlds of rhododendron and native azalea, past vineyards, and into a moist lowland area filled with lilies, cannas, and lotus. Look at fruiting hawthorns, the collection of more than sixty types of hosta, a fern forest, hollies, camellias in profusion, and a stand of a showy shrub called lily-of-the-valley bush. The iris collection contains more than six hundred different hybrids, and it's spectacular from April through July. Lantana, which grows wild in the southeast, is shown here in all its colors from deep orchid to blazing orange.

Beehives are placed beneath a water oak where visitors

can see the bees at work through a glass window. Junipers and three hundred other conifers fill another garden; the daylilies are a spectacle from June into early fall.

Take time to see and sniff the herb gardens and to study a trellis garden filled with vines such as kiwi, roses, passion flower, jasmine, and sweet pea. Returning to the entrance drive, see more than three hundred hybrid azaleas. Everything is caringly tended by a nonprofit foundation; everything is labeled, so it's a good place for laymen and black-thumb gardeners to get acquainted with Georgia's flora from the most common to the most exotic.

Where: On the east side of Business 441 South, Milledgeville. Open weekdays 8:30 A.M. to 4:30 P.M. and Saturday 1 to 5 P.M. Admission is free.
Facilities: Museum, restrooms.
For more information: Lockerly Arboretum, 1534 Irwinton Road, Milledgeville, GA 31061; 912-452-2112.

Massee Lane Gardens

These nine acres are the home of the American Camellia Society, so expect to find the brightest and best camellias blooming from late fall into the springtime under towering pine trees. In March and April, dogwood and azalea bloom to form canopies over narcissus, daffodils, and crocuses. Through the summer, iris, daylilies, Banksia roses, and hosts of other flowers make their appearance. During coldest weather, see what's going on in the greenhouse, too.

All seasons are right for contemplative walks through the Japanese garden, its pools glittering with golden koi. In two museums, see collections of Boehm porcelains and other objets d'art.

Where: Off State 49, five miles south of town. Admission.

Members and children under age twelve free. November through March, open Monday through Saturday 9 A.M. to 5 P.M. and Sunday 1 to 5 P.M. April through October, Monday to Friday 9 A.M. to 4 P.M.
Facilities: Gift shop, fifteen-minute slide presentation, restrooms.
For more information: Massee Lane Gardens, One Massee Lane, Fort Valley, GA 31030; 912-967-2722.

Marietta's Azalea and Dogwood Trails

The exact time for peak dogwood and azalea bloom can be different each year depending on temperatures and rainfall, but you can hardly go wrong in coming to Marietta in early to mid-April. By using the map provided by the Marietta Welcome Center, you'll see the best of the blooms as well as the Church-Cherokee National Register Historic District, which has more than a hundred and fifty historically significant structures. The route also passes through a more recent neighborhood called Oakton, once part of the original Oakton Plantation. Fair Oaks, on Kennesaw Avenue between Atwood Street and St. Marys Lane, is the home of the Marietta Educational Garden Center. Built in 1852, the home served as headquarters for Confederate General Joseph E. Johnston during the Battle of Kennesaw Mountain. The house and gardens have been restored to their original look and are open Monday, Wednesday, and Friday 10 A.M. to 2 P.M. Admission.

Where: Take exit 112 off I-75 and drive west on the South 120 Loop, following signs to the Welcome Center. From here, just follow the map you'll be given.
Special note: Cobb County's best private gardens are opened to the public for two days each May to benefit the Cobb Landmarks and Historical Society. It's a chance to see the South's favorite plants at their best, as well as unusual plantings and

landscape treatments. For dates and details, write to the Welcome Center.
For more information: Marietta Welcome Center, 4 Depot Street, Marietta, GA 30060; 404-429-1115. Stop in for a map or write ahead for driving maps to the Azalea and Dogwood Trails and the Historic Walking and Driving Tour.

Monastery of Our Lady the Holy Spirit

Here in a serene setting of duck ponds and farm fields, self-sufficient monks have been cultivating their gardens since 1944. Visitors are welcome to attend mass or prayer services and to picnic on the pleasant grounds during daylight hours. Don't miss the greenhouses with their bonsai collection.

Where: Eight miles southwest of Conyers via State 138/212. Call ahead for hours for greenhouse mass and prayer services. Shops closed Sunday.
Facilities: Picnic tables, bookstore, gift shop, homemade breads, tours, slide presentation.
For more information: Monastery of Our Lady the Holy Spirit, 2625 Highway 212, Conyers, GA 30207; 404-483-8705.

Noah's Ark

Leave I-75 at the Locust Grove exit (the village was named for its abundance of flowering locust trees) about twenty-five miles southeast of Atlanta to visit Noah's Ark, an animal rehabilitation center where six hundred injured native animals are being nurtured and healed with the hope of returning them to the wild.

Where: Noah's Ark, 1425 Locust Grove Road, Locust Grove, GA 30248; 404-957-0888. Open Friday and Saturday noon to 5 P.M.

Ocmulgee National Monument

For at least twelve thousand years, this 683-acre site on the Macon plains has been occupied by human families. A foot trail connects the scattered points of interest, most of them mysterious Indian mounds dating to the Mississippian culture of one thousand years ago. There's also a reconstructed Creek trading post. Hikers will want to leave the main trail to explore the Opelofa Nature Trail through the swampy lowlands of Walnut Creek.

Where: East of Macon on US 80.
Facilities: Museum, picnic area, restrooms, museum shop.
For more information: Superintendent's Office, Ocmulgee National Monument, 1207 Emery Highway, Macon, GA 31201. Call 912-477-3232 (the Museum of Arts and Sciences). Open daily 9 A.M. to 5 P.M. except Christmas and New Year's.

Oconee National Forest

Dwarfed by the dramatic, forested mountains of the Chattahoochee National Forest in north Georgia, Oconee National Forest is nevertheless a rich, natural treasure found in several noncontiguous plots in the rolling piedmont region between Athens and Macon.

Amethyst, feldspar, and granite are mined within the forest, and each year twenty million board feet of timber are harvested. Some of the pastures are opened sometimes for cattle grazing. The forest is the home of such endangered species as the bald eagle and the red-cockaded woodpecker and of more common species, including skunk, possum, raccoon, rabbit, squirrel, trophy-size deer, and wild turkey. In all, about three hundred and fifty species of animals and fish have been identified here, plus about fifteen hundred plant species.

Skunks

More than fifty hunting and fishing camps within the forest are equipped with fire rings, pit toilets, and a parking area. Within the 113,000-acre forest are half a dozen developed recreation areas, most of them on the waters of the Oconee and Ocmulgee Rivers or on lakes formed by the damming of rivers. They include:

Dyar Pasture Boat Ramp. Launch a canoe or other small boat on this remote stretch of Lake Oconee in a waterfowl conservation area. Take your binoculars to look for loons, grebes, herons, and a long list of ducks. From the parking lot, look for hiking trails into the conservation area.

It's eight miles west of Greensboro on State 278; go right on Greshamville Road one mile, then right on Copeland Road. After two miles, cross Greenbriar Creek, then go one-eighth mile to a right turn onto a dirt road to the ramp.

Redlands Boat Ramp is also on Lake Oconee. From Greensboro, take State 278 west six miles, then go south on Forest Service Road 1255 for a mile to the boat ramp.

Swords Boat Ramp gives access to yet another scrawny finger of massive Lake Oconee. Take State 278 west from Greensboro for six and a half miles, then go south on County 1135 for four miles.

Oconee River Park nestles in the piedmont area in natural contours along the river. It's equipped for camping, fishing, and picnicking and has marked hiking trails. Drive west from Greensboro for twelve miles on State 15 and find it along the highway.

Scull Shoals was once a prosperous community along the river, but nothing remains today except fragments and foundations of Georgia's first paper mill, one of the first cotton gins, a textile mill, and the remains of dozens of homes and factories. Hike to the area from a mile-long trail that begins at the boat ramp on the river along State 15 or take Macedonia Church Road and go left on Forest Service Road 1234 and left again on Forest Service Road 1231.

Hillsboro Lake is a delightful little pool surrounded by woodlands. Bring a picnic lunch and a fishing rod. From Hillsboro, drive southeast on the paved country road for three miles.

Lake Sinclair straggles south from Lake Oconee, adding another 15,000 sparkling acres to one of the state's best recreation resources. The home of Joel Chandler Harris, who wrote the Uncle Remus stories, is on US 441 in nearby Eatonton. The park has campsites, boating, fishing, picnic tables, and a swimming area. Take US 129 south from Eatonton for ten

miles, then go left (east) on State 212 for a mile, left on Forest Service Road 1062 for two miles, and follow signs to the lake.
For more information on all the above sites: Oconee Ranger District, 349 Forsyth Road, Monticello, GA 31064; 706-468-2244.

Panola Mountain State Conservation Park

The hundred-acre granite monadnock here is often compared to Stone Mountain near Atlanta, but it's unique. In this unquarried, undisturbed outcropping, you'll find rare piedmont plants and animals that aren't found on sister mountains Stone and Arabia. A National Natural Landmark, the park covers 617 acres of rocky slopes, streams, a little lake, hardwood forests, swamps, and grassy meadows.

The habitat, thinly covered by soil over granite, is a fragile one telling an eloquent story of fifteen million years of evolution that began when the first plants got a foothold on the rock and released weak acids that began to break down the rock. Over the millennia, an ever-deepening soil bed gave rise to daisies, sparkleberry, and finally forests.

Where: Eighteen miles southeast of Atlanta on State 155. Take exit 36 off I-20. Park hours vary winter and summer, but generally follow daylight hours. Interpretive Center hours are 9 A.M. to 5 P.M., Tuesday to Friday; noon to 5 P.M., Saturday and Sunday.
Facilities: Picnic tables, picnic shelter, interpretive center with rest-rooms. Self-guided nature trails, fitness trail, guided mountain hikes on weekends, educational programs (including spring and fall wildflower walks), and environmental discovery programs in summer for children ages five to thirteen.
For more information: Panola Mountain State Conservation Park, 2600 Highway 155 S.W., Stockbridge, GA 30281; 770-389-7801.

Piccadilly Farm

This is a working farm where visitors are welcome to stroll gardens and nurseries that spill over with Georgia's favorite blooms. Your hosts, Sam and Carleen Jones and Jeff Dawson, are in the business of selling plants, but they also delight in showing browsers around. The perennials' displays range from acanthus and six types of ajuga to half a dozen phlox and four verbenas. Ferns and Lenten roses are a specialty, and they have hostas in more than a hundred colors!

Where: Off State 53 near Watkinsville. Turn on Elder Road at Oconee County Park and follow the signs.

For more information: Piccadilly Farm, 1971 Whipporwill Road, Bishop, GA 30621; 706-769-6516. Visitors admitted only during retail sale days, which vary with the season. In spring, generally early April to mid-June, an educational garden stroll is offered at 10:30 A.M. on Saturdays. It's essential to call ahead.

Piedmont National Wildlife Refuge

Old trees and woodpeckers are once more reigning over a 35,000-acre refuge that by the Great Depression had been reduced almost to dust-bowl status by war, erosion, abuse, abandonment, and the boll weevil. Today, loblolly pines once again grow on the ridges while hardwoods reclaim the creek bottoms and slopes. Red-cockaded woodpeckers, an endangered species whose habitat had been all but destroyed, once again have a home. Warblers, chickadees, and nuthatches sing again while wild turkeys, wood ducks, and great blue herons strut the recovering wetlands. Even a few bluebirds might be seen.

Come in January to enjoy the cool, insect-free days and to watch for Canada geese and golden eagles. By February, deer range to the edges of the woodlands to look for food while wood ducks nest in the boxes set out for them. Wintering

Red-cockaded woodpecker

birds begin to fly north as trees swell with buds and pine pollen gilds everything with a sneezy blanket.

Summer birds are nesting by April, when the migrations are at their best. Flowering shrubs are in full trumpet, and turtles begin to venture out to sunbathe on fallen logs. By

May, box turtles are nesting while bobwhites begin to mate and brood. June and July turn hot, buzzing with insects and aflitter with fledglings leaving their nests. Still and humid, August is a time for watching for wading birds and watching out for ticks. Be sure to get a tick repellent; mosquito sprays alone won't do.

A breath of cool air brings waves of migratory birds. Bold deer and wild turkeys may be seen in autumn along the paths, while pawpaw and wild grapes turn sweet and sticky with juices that are irresistible to animals, birds, and hungry bugs of all sizes and colors.

With the fall, migrating birds continue to arrive, some to stay and others to continue to South America. Seasonal floods bring duck season; deer are in velvet; hardwoods put on their prettiest colors. December, cold and quiet, is a time for beavers to continue their search for twigs as raptors soar overhead.

Come any time of year to rejoice in this nonstop nature show. Hunting and fishing have seasons; visitors are welcome any time during daylight hours. A two-and-a-half-mile woodpecker trail goes through a colony of endangered red-cockaded woodpeckers, which can be seen nesting in May and June.

The mile-long Allison Lake Trail wanders through bottomlands and forests along the lake, where you can see beaver dams across Allison Creek. The Little Rock Wildlife Drive is a six-mile gravel road that can be self-guided with the aid of a free booklet picked up at the office.

Bring your binoculars and a bird identification book. A long list of birds are seen all year, including the great blue heron, great egret, vulture, pied-billed grebe, belted kingfisher, and red-bellied woodpecker. With luck, you may spot a purple gallinule in summer, a horned lark in fall or winter, or a magnolia warbler in springtime. All are uncommon but have been identified here.

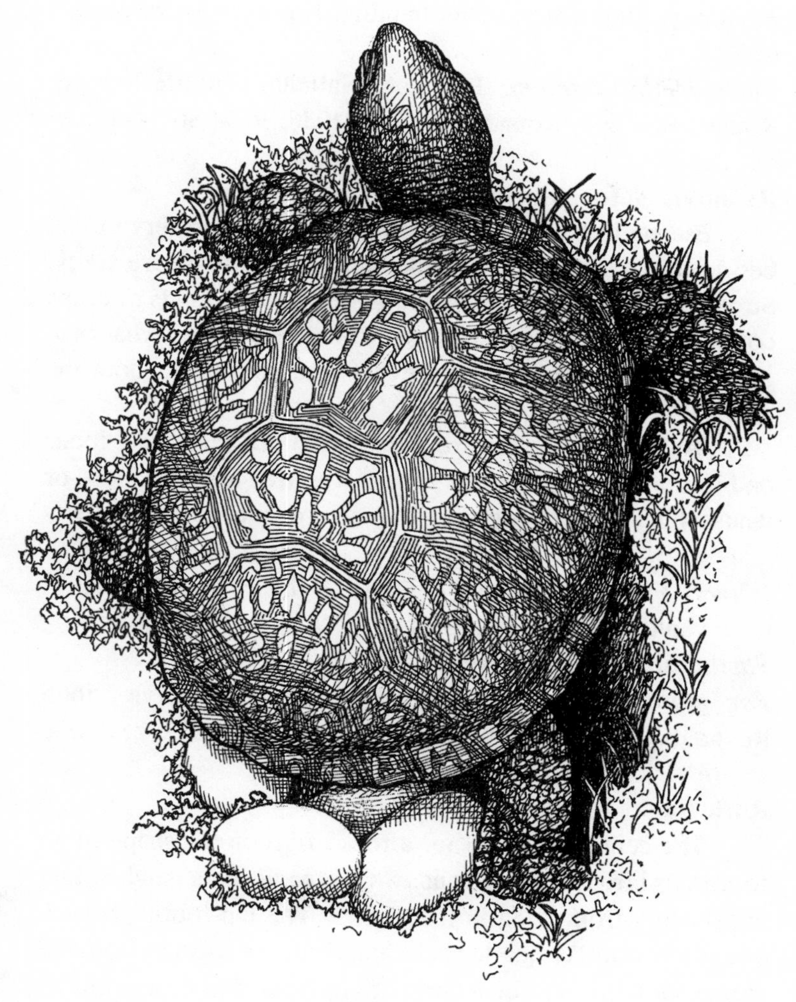

Box turtle

Where: Take exit 61 off I-75, then go east on Julette Road for eighteen miles to the visitors center. Or take State 11 between Gray and Monticello. Just north of Round Oak, go west on the paved road for three miles to the office.

Facilities: Limited camping, hunting, fishing, visitors center, trails.
For more information: Piedmont National Wildlife Refuge, Route 1 Box 670, Round Oak, GA 31038; 912-986-5441.

Reynolds Nature Preserve

Escape to the leafy cool of this 130-acre preserve to sit beside the Azalea Pond or hike four miles of nature trails. Stroll the herb and vegetable gardens to see the kinds of crops commonly grown a century ago. Call ahead to see what programs are scheduled; special events are held throughout the year.

Visitors of all ages are welcome to programs that focus on birds, mammals, reptiles, insect life, tree identification, or landscaping. Some programs include a picnic, jog, or hike.

Where: From I-75, take Old Dixie Highway US 19/41 north to Reynolds Roads, then go east.
Facilities: Picnic area, restrooms.
For more information: Reynolds Nature Preserve, 5665 Reynolds Road, Morrow, GA 30260; 404-9619257.

Rock Eagle 4-H Center

The center is named for a rock effigy in the shape of an enormous bird, a hundred and two feet long and a hundred and twenty feet from wingtip to wingtip. The ten-foot-high rock pile made of milky quartz rocks and boulders appears from the observation tower to be a bird with its head facing east, but its ancient origins are a mystery. When the first white settlers arrived, the Indians knew only that the bird had been found there by their ancestors. It's thought to date back six thousand years to the Old Quartz Industry period.

A national historic landmark, the site is a conference center for 4-H. Find lodgings and dining in Eatonton.

Where: Between Madison and Eatonton on State 441/129, twelve miles from I-20.
Facilities: Restrooms, hiking trails, observation tower (open during daylight hours; free), use of the 110-acre lake. Groups of eighteen to eleven hundred can also book lodgings, meals, meeting rooms, golf, and swimming.
For more information: Rock Eagle, 350 Rock Eagle Road, Eatonton, GA 31024; 706-485-2831.

State Botanical Garden of Georgia

Every day is springtime inside the conservatory, but in the outdoors April and May are irresistible times to hike five miles of trails through 313 acres of gardens abloom with native azalea and dogwood. Ramble under huge magnolia trees and walk along the banks of the Middle Oconee River. A tram system is in the planning, but for now footpaths lead visitors through an Eden of rhododendrons, the dahlia garden, an herb garden, a shade garden, a native flora section, a trial garden, a rock garden, and flourishing plantings of bright annuals, all accented with picturesque plazas.

Where: 2450 South Milledge Avenue, on the river in Athens. From downtown Athens, go south on Milledge Avenue, the main street, about five miles. The complex is open Monday to Saturday 9:00 A.M. to 4:30 P.M., Sundays 11:30 A.M. to 4:30 P.M. except some holidays.
Facilities: The café serves lunch daily from 11:30 A.M. to 2:00 P.M. Restrooms, pay phones, and first aid are available in the Callaway Building and Visitor Center.
For more information: Call 706-542-6151.

State Farmers Market

The largest market of its kind in the world, this is nature's theme park filled with the freshest harvest from around this bounteous state and throughout the nation. No mere tourist attraction, this is a throbbing, enormous wholesale market filled with the roar of trucks and the slap of loading and unloading. Visitors are welcome to look and to buy every day, twenty-four hours a day.

Where: Ten miles south of Atlanta. Take the Forest Parkway exit off I-75. Open twenty-four hours daily.
For more information: Atlanta Convention and Visitors Bureau, 233 Peachtree Street N.E. Suite 2000, Atlanta, GA 30303; 404-521-6600.

Sandy Creek Nature Center

Nature trails wind through two hundred acres of mixed forests, boggy lowlands, and meadows. Children like to talk to the animals and go through an original log cabin that is almost two hundred years old.

Where: North of the Athens bypass off US 442 a half mile.
Facilities: Sandy Creek Park nearby has primitive camping, picnicking, playgrounds, game fields, swimming, boating, tennis courts.
For more information: Convention and Visitors Bureau, 220 College Avenue, Athens, GA 30601; 706-546-1805.

The Tree That Owns Itself

It's a pleasant little legend, and a majestic oak that makes a good backdrop for souvenir photos. The land was owned by Col. William H. Jackson, a professor at the University of Georgia, who so loved his big shade tree that he recorded a deed giving eight feet of land around the tree to the tree itself. When a storm blew the tree down in 1942, the Junior Ladies' Garden Club planted a sapling, which was grown from acorns of the original tree, on the site. Today, the mature oak still stands sentinel atop the hill, on land it owns.

Where: The corner of Dearing and Finey Streets in Athens.
Facilities: None.
For more information: Convention and Visitors Bureau, 220 College Avenue, Athens, GA 30603; 706-546-1805.

Stone Mountain Park

Passengers who fly into Atlanta are always awed by the sight of this huge lump in the landscape, and it has become a favorite playground for Atlantans. A 3,200-acre park surrounds the largest mass of exposed granite in the world. Some nature lovers will be put off by the commercialism surrounding the mountain and the Civil War carving on its face, but the hoopla centers only in some areas and there are still many hidden pockets of uncrowded wilderness. Nightly laser shows are held at 9:30 P.M. through the summer.

Where: Take the Stone Mountain exit off US 78. A daily or annual parking permit is required, and admission is charged for some activities.
Facilities: Picnicking, shows, food service, sightseeing, restrooms, talking trails.
For more information: Georgia's Stone Mountain Park, Highway 78, Stone Mountain, GA 30086; 404-498-5702.

Vines Botanical Gardens

The twenty-five developed acres of a regal, ninety-acre estate have been developed around the stately manor home and a lake with fountains.

Where: On Oak Grove Road in Loganville.

For more information: Vines Botanical Gardens, Oak Grove Road, Loganville, GA 30249; 404-466-7532.

Wild Birds Unlimited

Although this is a retail store, it will beguile any nature lover who wants to learn more about backyard bird feeding. On sale here are no-waste birdseed blends, feeders, hardware and birdhouses, nature books, and much more.

Where: Wild Birds Unlimited, 2139A Roswell Road N.E., Marietta, GA 30062; 404-565-9841. Open daily, daylight hours.

Yellow River Wildlife Game Ranch

Walk the rambling trail to meet wildlife as you go. There are always animals to see, others to pet.

Where: East of Atlanta on US 78.
For more information: Yellow River Wildlife Game Ranch, 4525 Highway 78, Lilburn, GA 30247; 770-972-6643. Admission.

Zoo Atlanta

Most visitors head straight for the African Rain Forest, where more than a dozen gorillas cavort and cut up to the delight of visitors of all ages. The zoo presents more than a thousand creatures in natural habitats. The children's zoo has an OK-to-Touch Corral, a playground, and a tram that is fun to ride as well as a step-saver.

Hours: 10 A.M. to 5 P.M. daily; until 6 P.M. daily during daylight savings time. Closed Christmas, New Year's, Martin Luther King Day, and Thanksgiving. Admission.

Where: Half a mile south of exit 26 off I-20 east of downtown, in Grant Park. On MARTA, take a No. 31, 32, or 97 bus or (summer only) the Zoo Trolley from the Five Points rail station.
Facilities: Tram, restrooms, food service, playground, picnic area.
For more information: Zoo Atlanta, 800 Cherokee Avenue S.E., Atlanta, GA 30303; 404-624-5600. Admission.

8

Northwest Mountains

One of Georgia's best-kept tourism secrets is its mountains, perhaps because most outsiders associate Georgia more with antebellum mansions or the Colonial Coast. Or perhaps because they picture the Blue Ridge and Smoky Mountains only in Virginia, Tennessee, and North Carolina.

Make no mistake. Georgia's wilderness mountains, rising to a crescendo from the piedmont region northwest of Atlanta and climaxing at Lookout Mountain just across the Tennessee border, are magnificent.

These mountains are laced with creeks and rushing streams, including, farther east, the legendary Chattooga. A waterfall awaits around almost every bend in the trail. Steeply forested hillsides are reigned over by bald eagles. Almost the entire Northwest Mountain Region is within a wildlife management area, a state park, the Chattahoochee National Forest, or all of the above.

Barnsley Gardens

The beauties of the boxwood gardens lay forgotten for years around the remains of Woodlands, an antebellum cotton empire. Now the ragged ruins, which have been stabilized and floored but remain open, brood over old gardens and ferneries that have been restored to the way they may have been when ladies in hoop skirts strolled their cool pathways.

Walk through the formal garden with its twelve-foot fountain and view of the old mansion where dashing Godfrey Barnsley brought his bride, Julia Scarborough. The garden was his gift to her, and he continued to add exotic plants brought from his travels all over the world. He is credited with introducing the Green Rose to the south. The romantic story ended when Julia died young, the Civil War came to the doorstep of Woodlands, and Godfrey died penniless in 1873.

Amble into the wildflower meadow, the fernery, through the rhododendrons and roses, and past the ponds and perennials. Look closely and you'll find the gravestone of a Confederate soldier, perhaps killed in a cavalry skirmish that occurred here and was pictured in *Harper's Weekly*, July 2, 1864.

The stately homes of England are known for their great expanses of green lawns, formal gardens, artfully placed ponds and pathways, with a bit of sculpture here and a fountain there. The scene has been replicated here in northwest Georgia where British-born Godfrey Barnsley built his cotton empire in the 1840s in the manner worthy of American royalty. Fittingly, the estate is now owned by Prince Hubertus Fugger and his wife, Princess Alexandra, of Bavaria.

Barnsley's travels as a cotton king took him all over the world, where he collected bulbs and cuttings to create his landmark garden. He's credited with introducing the Green Rose to the South; today, more than two hundred varieties still bloom in the rose gardens.

After the Civil War, Barnsley died widowed and penniless and his lands languished, but his legacy thrives again on sixteen hundred grandly restored acres. Borders of blooms surround woodland gardens, ferneries, ponds peppered with waterlilies, oceans of rhododendrons and azaleas, and a grand boxwood parterre garden centered around a twelve-foot fountain. The original plantation home, destroyed by a storm in 1906, has been stabilized and now stands as a stark ruin against the meticulously groomed grounds. It's a year-round showplace starting with azaleas in spring, rhododendrons in early summer, blazing red sourwood in fall, and camellias in the cold of winter.

Where: Between Adairsville and Kingston, about sixty miles north of Atlanta. From I-75, take exit 128 and go west on State 140 for one and a half miles, then go left on Hall Station Road for five and a half miles to Barnsley Gardens Road, then two and a half miles and turn left. The route is well signed.

Admission. Open February to mid-December. Tuesday through Saturday 10 A.M. to 5 P.M. Sunday noon to 5 P.M. Closed Mondays and mid-December through January.

Facilities: Café, gift shop, picnic area, restrooms, museum.

For more information: Barnsley Gardens, 597 Barnsley Gardens Road, Adairsville, GA 30103; 404-773-7480.

Berry College

Berry College is one of the most unusual colleges in the United States, a "miracle in the mountains" in which students learn marketable skills while living and working on a campus that is almost completely self-sufficient. Founded by Martha Berry for poor mountain children, the school has become a showplace of academic excellence, superb crafts, and stately, Oxford-inspired buildings funded by Henry Ford.

Its natural wonders begin with the forested mountains

themselves and spread through acres of formal and informal gardens, farm fields, experimental crops, and native and exotic plantings. Pick up an audio tape and take the self-guided tour.

Where: Highway 27 North at Georgia Loop 1.
Facilities: Museum, art gallery, restrooms.
For more information: Oakhill and the Martha Berry Museum, Highway 27 North at Georgia Loop 1, Rome, GA 30149; 706-291-1883.

Cave Spring

A prosperous community sprang up two hundred years ago around a mineral spring that gushes pure, cold water from a deep limestone cave into a pond that pours into a 1.5-acre swimming pool. The spring is open to the public in summer. So are many of the area's mansions, ninety of which are listed on the National Register of Historic Places.

Where: Southwest of Rome ten miles on US 441.
Facilities: Swimming pool, picnic area, gift shops, historic sites.
For more information: The Chamber of Commerce, Cave Spring, GA 30124; 706-777-3382.

Cloudland Canyon State Park

One of the greatest pleasures of touring Georgia's natural treasures is to choose from a menu that ranges from sugar-sand Atlantic beaches to misty mountains. Here in Cloudland Canyon, which is actually the western edge of Chattanooga's famous Lookout Mountain, you're as close to heaven as a rugged climb can carry you.

Straddling a deep gorge that was cut into the mountain by Sitton Gulch Creek, the 2,120-acre park beckons hikers to six miles of back-country trails leading to flashing waterfalls, cloud-high lookouts, and breathtaking gorges.

Where: Take exit 2 (Trenton) off I-59 and go east on State 136 to the park entrance.
Facilities: Tent and trailer campsites, cottages, tennis courts, swimming pool, walk-in campsites, picnic tables with grills, hiking trails.
For more information: Cloudland Canyon State Park, Route 2, Box 150, Rising Fawn, GA 30738; 706-657-4050.

Cohutta Wilderness

A separate island of wilderness that is not connected to other segments of the Chattahoochee National Forest, this 34,500-acre reservation is part of the forest nevertheless. It is threaded with seventy miles of forest trails, two state highways, and the tumbling Conasauga River. Cohutta Wilderness is a favorite with hikers and llama trekkers.

Where: Take State 71 north from Dalton. The Cohutta's main east-west road is State 2. For llama-trekking information, contact the Convention and Visitors Bureau, 2211 Dug Gap Battle Road, Dalton, GA 30720; 706-272-7676.
For more information: Get maps from the Cohutta Ranger District, 401 Old Ellijay Road, Chatsworth, GA 30705; 706-695-6736.

Fort Mountain State Park

The ancient, 855-foot rock wall on the highest point of this mountain was probably a fortification, and it was built long before Columbus. This park, part of the Chattahoochee National Forest near the Cohutta Wilderness, has twelve miles of foot trails and an eight-and-two-tenths-mile back-country trail for hiking or backpacking.

Where: Seven miles east of Chatsworth via State 52.
For more information: Fort Mountain State Park, Route 7, Box 7008, Chatsworth, GA 30705; 706-695-2621.

Keown Falls

Even during those few times when this charming little waterfall is dry, it's worth the drive to this scenic area in the valleys and ridges of the Chattahoochee National Forest. Skittering squirrels and chipmunks divert attention from the silent passing of white-tailed deer and elusive wild turkeys. Bring a picnic lunch and hike the hills and dales.

Turkey hen

Where: Drive east on State 136 from LaFayette for thirteen and a half miles through Villanow, then go right on Pocket Road for about five miles to the entrance to the Keown Falls Scenic Area.
For more information: Armuchee Ranger District, 806 East Villanow Street, Lafayette, GA 30728; 706-638-1085.

Lake Conasauga

This is the highest lake in Georgia, nestled in the green mountains and reminiscent of the Adirondacks or the Rockies. It's a tiny, nineteen-acre pocket of serenity where the only motors allowed are electric. Along the way, you'll pass Barnes Creek, where you can picnic along a stream that has a small waterfall.

Where: Take US 411 north from Chatsworth for four miles, then go east (right) at the traffic light in Eton and follow Forest Road 18 east for ten miles. Turn northeast (left) on Forest Service Road 68 and go ten miles more.
Facilities: Camping, picnic sites, hiking trails, boating, swimming.
For more information: Cohutta Ranger District, 401 Old Ellijay Road, Chatsworth, GA 30705; 706-695-6736.

Lithia Springs

Only three springs in the world contain lithium, which nineteenth-century doctors praised for its healing powers. Today, this historic spring still spews its miracle waters, which are bottled and sold here. Visitors are welcome to see the medicinal garden, grounds, and Family Doctor Museum, all of them free.

Where: Go west from Atlanta on I-20 to the second Six Flags exit (12, Thornton Road), then count eight traffic lights to

Bankhead. Turn right and look for Lithia Springs after two hundred feet on your right.
Facilities: Fast food nearby. Restrooms, museum, medicinal garden, bottled lithia water for sale.
For more information: Lithia Springs, Box 713, Lithia Springs, GA 30057; 706-944-3880.

Marshall Forest

The first National Natural Landmark in the state, this 250-acre virgin woodland displays typical mountain hardwoods and evergreens on a carpet of fallen leaves, pine needles, and wildflowers. Tornadoes and hurricane-force snow storms in the early 1990s put the forest through nature's severest pruning. To retain its natural state, preservationists have left fallen trees as they were. Evolving in nature's inexorable way, it remains a natural wonder in the heart of the city.

Where: Off Georgia 20W on Horseleg Creek Road.
Facilities: The forest has a braille trail.
For more information: Friends of Marshall Forest, c/o Dr. Mark Knaufs, Shorter College, 315 Shorter Avenue, Rome, GA 30165; 706-291-2121, ext. 205.
Note: Entering Rome, note the Welcome Center in a restored 1901 railroad depot. It's open daily 10 A.M. to 4 or 5 P.M., staffed by knowledgeable volunteers who go the extra mile to offer Southern hospitality. Ask for maps, directions, information on lodging and meals.

Red Top Mountain State Park

Named for the red, iron-rich soil that was once mined here, this highly developed park fills a 1,950-acre peninsula in Lake Allatoona. Most people come for the swimming, boating, and fishing, but you can get away from the throngs by striking out on the seven miles of nature trails to look for remnants of old iron mines.

Where: Two miles east of I-75 via exit 123.
For more information: Red Top Mountain State Park, 653 Red Top Mountain Road S.E., Cartersville, GA 30120; 706-975-0055.

Sweetwater Creek State Conservation Area

Five miles of hiking trails through woods and waters now cover the area where a Civil War-era textile mill once stood along Sweetwater Creek. The ruins can still be seen here. Fish in the lake or streams, plug into a ranger-led nature program, or make your own survey of mountain songbirds, flowering trees, and wildflowers.

Where: Take I-20 west from Atlanta, exit at Thornton Road, and go left a quarter of a mile. Turn right onto Blairs Bridge Road, then left onto Mount Vernon Road, following signs to the park.
For more information: Sweetwater Creek State Conservation Park, Box 816, Lithia Springs, GA 30057; 706-944-1700.

William Weinman Mineral Museum

Founded by the family of William Weinman, who pioneered barite mining in the Cartersville area, this mineral museum is a favorite with tourists as well as a gathering spot for rockhounds. On display are more than five thousand fossils, gems, and minerals in three exhibit halls. Also shown are Indian artifacts as old as the Archaic period, circa 8,000 B.C. Larger specimens are outdoors in the mineral garden, where antique mining equipment is on display.

Where: Take exit 126 off I-75, then go southwest on US 411

to Mineral Museum Drive, Cartersville, GA 30120. Admission. Open Tuesday to Saturday 10 A.M. to 4:30 P.M., Sunday 2 to 4:30 P.M. Closed Mondays and major holidays. Free admission during annual Rock Swap, second Saturday in June.
Facilities: Research facilities, lectures, teacher workshops, mineral identification, handicapped access, gift shop.
For more information: Call 706-386-0576.

Special Events

Most of these events have no admission charge, although standard state park fees apply to events that are held in state parks. While admission is free to most festivals, additional fees may be charged for special concerts or displays, and most families will also want to have cash on hand for food, arts and crafts, games, and other temptations.

Food, family, and fireworks festivals occur almost every weekend somewhere in Georgia. Listed here are only those festivals that have to do with the natural wonders of Georgia. For a list of additional fairs and festivals that give you a special reason to drive into the Peachtree State's scenic mountains, bountiful plains, verdant woodlands, or some forgotten hamlet, call 800-VISIT-GA.

March

Macon's annual Cherry Blossom Festival attracts half a million people to see the splendor of almost two hundred thousand cherry trees in bloom. Ceremonies, parades, antebellum-home tours, hot-air balloons, a street party, fireworks, an international foods fair, a coronation ball, and music from rock to country, jazz to gospel. 912-751-7429.

Savannah's annual Tour of Homes and Gardens is one of the South's premier tours and a rare opportunity to see behind the garden gates of mansions that are usually closed to the public. 912-233-7706. Admission.

Tybee Island's annual Kitefest fills the sky with color while visitors enjoy the beach breezes. Fly a kite for fun or prizes, take a kite-flying lesson, or just watch. 912-232-7201.

Wildflower Day is observed at Crooked River State Park near St. Marys. Lowland wildflowers typical of moist and marshy subtropics flourish here. 912-882-5256.

March/April

Conyers' Cherry Blossom Watching goes on for almost an entire month when its one thousand Yoshino cherry trees come into flower. Japanese guests and exchange students join in the celebration; cherry trees may be purchased. 770-918-2169.

April

Spring wildflower walks are conducted at Panola Mountain State Conservation Park, Stockbridge. 404-389-7801.

Gray is the setting for the Jones County Wildlife Festival. In Georgia, where the harvest of game is a time-honored practice, a festival means the eating of deer, turkey, rabbit, and squirrel as well as a petting zoo and live animal displays, contests, and crafts. 912-986-5052.

Mossy Creek Barnyard is a celebration of old-time crafts, song, and stories under the pines near Perry. 912-922-8265.

Oatland Island's "Tour of Homes" is a take-off on the famous Tour of Homes and Gardens in nearby Savannah, except this time the homes are the animal habitats at the island's education center. 800-444-2427. Admission.

Hidden Gardens of Historic Savannah tour is even more of a must-see than the homes-and-gardens tour in March. The most beautiful walled gardens are singled out for landscape design, ironwork, art, and uniqueness. The event includes a mansion tour and afternoon tea. Fee. 912-238-0248.

Special wildflower programs herald springtime at Vogel State Park, Blairsville. Come to photograph spring flowers and to hear legends of Indian battles and gold strikes. 706-745-2628. Wildflower Weekend is in late April at Steven C. Foster State Park, Fargo, 912-637-5274.

May

Atlanta Botanical Garden is a natural wonder at any time, but especially in early May during its annual Gardens for Connoisseurs Tour, because the most unusual plants and gardens are featured. 404-876-5859. Admission.

Mountain Laurel Festival, Clarkesville. Come to see the historic downtown area or simply drive the surrounding mountainsides, which are alight with laurel in bloom. 404-778-4654.

Wildflower Festival of the Arts, Dahlonega, comes at the best time for spring mountain-flower viewing. Take quiet nature walks or enjoy the arts and entertainments around the historic town square. 706-864-3711.

July

The prunifolia azalea season is at Callaway Gardens. 800-282-8181.

August

Astronomy evenings are scheduled at Florence Marina State Park, Omaha. Come to scan the sky from the northern end of Lake Walter F. George on the Chattahoochee River. 912-838-4244.

Georgia Indian Awareness Weekend is observed at Watson Mill Bridge State Park, Comer. Come to enjoy the placid mill pond, century-old wooden bridge, picnicking under the trees, and an assembling of Indian tribes. 706-783-5349.

Kudzu Takeover Day is celebrated at Providence Canyon State Conservation Park, seven miles west of Lumpkin. The humor is tongue-in-cheek, but kudzu, an imported vine that can grow more than a foot a day, is a mixed blessing in Georgia. Planted as a ground cover, it can take over acres of land in a year. 912-838-6202.

Old Timers Day is observed at Vogel State Park, Blairsville, one of the oldest state parks in Georgia. 706-745-2628.

September

Lakeland's Flatlanders Arts and Crafts Show on the banks of the Alapaha River is a small-town festival in a natural setting miles from anywhere. Come to camp, fish, listen to bluegrass and gospel, shop for country crafts, sample home-made local sausage. Write Flatlanders, Box 125, Lakeland, GA 31636; 912-842-3463.

Fall wildflower walks at Panola Mountain State Conservation Park, Stockbridge, take advantage both of brilliant leaves as the trees change and of the bright golds and reds of seasonal wildflowers. 404-389-7801.

Stone Mountain sets up a festival for those who come to see seas of rare Confederate yellow daisies bloom this month. 404-498-5702.

Riverfest is an excellent excuse to loll along the banks of the Etowah River in Boling Park, Canton. Food, family events, and a special area for children. 706-479-5601.

October

"Indigo, A Colonial Export" is a yearly program that focuses on an important colonial crop used for dyes. It's held at Fort Morris Historic Site, Midway. 912-884-5999.

Mossy Creek Barnyard is a celebration of old-time crafts, songs, and stories under Georgia pines near Perry. 912-922-8265.

The yearly Sorghum Festival at Blairsville features the pungent syrup that is pressed from sorghum cane on a donkey-driven mill and boiled down to sticky sweetness. 706-745-5789.

Sunbelt Agricultural Exposition in Moultrie is the largest farm show in the Southeast. See crops, foods, equipment, demonstrations, and visitors from all over the world. 912-386-3459.

December

The buzzards return to the leafless trees of Reed Bingham State Park and can be seen in clusters and even entire communities against the stark winter sky. Shoo the blues at a rollicking Buzzard Festival. 912-727-2339.

Index

Titles in the Natural Wonders Series:

Natural Wonders of Alaska ($9.95)
Natural Wonders of Connecticut & Rhode Island ($9.95)
Natural Wonders of Florida ($9.95)
Natural Wonders of Georgia ($9.95)
Natural Wonders of Idaho ($9.95)
Natural Wonders of Massachusetts ($9.95)
Natural Wonders of Michigan ($9.95)
Natural Wonders of Minnesota ($9.95)
Natural Wonders of New Hampshire ($9.95)
Natural Wonders of New Jersey ($9.95)
Natural Wonders of New York ($9.95)
Natural Wonders of Northern California ($9.95)
Natural Wonders of Ohio ($9.95)
Natural Wonders of Oregon ($12.95)
Natural Wonders of Southern California ($9.95)
Natural Wonders of Tennessee ($9.95)
Natural Wonders of Texas ($9.95)
Natural Wonders of Vermont ($12.95)
Natural Wonders of Virginia ($9.95)
Natural Wonders of Washington ($12.95)
Natural Wonders of Wisconsin ($9.95)

Available at bookstores
or by ordering direct from the
publisher (please add $3.00
for shipping and handling).
Prices subject to change.

Country Roads Press
P.O. Box 838
Oaks, PA 19456